In Search of the Treasure of Faith

CFI Book Division
Gordonsville, Tennessee USA

In Search of the Treasure of Faith

"Go in quest of knowledge, even to China."
"The ink of the scholar is more holy than the blood of the martyr."
"The acquisition of knowledge is a duty incumbent on every Muslim, male and female." (Sayings of Muhammad)

"And fight them till the mischief of servitude to other than Allah, is annihilated, and the worship is completely for Allah alone."
(*The Qur'an*, 8:39)

Robert J. Wieland

Copyright © 2020 by CFI Book Division
Cover and interior design by CFI Graphic Design
All Rights Reserved. No part of this book may be reproduced in any form or by any electronic or mechanical means including information storage and retrieval systems without permission from its publisher, CFI Book Division.

Unless otherwise noted Bible quotations are from King James Version, copyright ©1988, B. B. Kirkebride Bible Company, Inc., Indianapolis, Indiana; used by permission.
TEV *Good News Translation*, copyright ©1976, permission given by the American Bible Society.
NIV *New International Version*, copyright ©1978, permission given by New York International Bible Society.

Published by CFI Book Division
P.O. Box 159, Gordonsville, Tennessee 38563

ISBN-13: 978-1-7344387-1-0

Printed in the Great Britain
Typeset in 12/14.8 Bembo Book MT Std

In the Name of Allah
The Beneficent, the Merciful

Praise Be to Allah, Lord of the Worlds

The Beneficent, the Merciful
Owner of the Day of Judgment

Thee (Alone) We Worship:

Thee (Alone) We Ask For Help

Show Us the Straight Path
The Path of Those
Whom Thou Hast Favoured

Not (the Path) of Those
Who Earn Thine Anger

Nor of Those Who Go Astray

Contents

1. The Thrill of Discovering Buried Treasure............. 9
2. Our Tospy-Turvy World Needs True Religion 15
3. Abraham's Islam................................. 21
4. Abraham's Faith Astonishes the World 29
5. How Abraham Became "The Friend of God".......... 39
6. Good News: Allah Shows a Smiling Face! 49
7. Allah's Way to Health, Happiness, and Longer Life 61
8. Can We Know What Lies Beyond Death?............. 75
9. The Great War Behind All Wars: Satan's Hatred
   Against Allah 87
10. Why Allah Commanded Hazrat Abraham
    to Offer His Son................................ 99
11. Who Is Jesus Christ (Sayyidna Al Masih)?............ 111
12. The Man Who Bore the Mysterious Curse of God,
    and Yet Lived 129
13. The Return of Jesus and the End of the World........ 143
14. Allah's True Covenant of Sabbath Rest.............. 159
15. The Mystery of How Sunday Observance Began...... 171
16. Finding Peace of Mind and Heart 187
17. The Daily, Practical Life of Faith 199
    Appendix A 205
    Appendix B 211

"You will not attain unto piety until you sacrifice for God all that is dear to you."
(*The Qur'an*, 3:92).

1
The Thrill of Discovering Buried Treasure

Ali appeared to have lost his mind. His wife, children, neighbours, and relatives could not fathom the reason for his strange doings.

He had always been a hard-working father, trying to provide for his family and save what he could of his meagre earnings. He treasured what few possessions he had. When he was able to buy his wife some fancy new clothes, his face would glow like a light shining in an alabaster bowl while he watched her display them. His smile was like a sunrise as he watched his children enjoy some new toy or a special sweet he was able to buy for them.

But what has come into him now? Is he demented?

First, he has sold his faithful donkey, on which he depends for his daily livelihood, and his cart as well. Next, he has gathered up all his own clothes and rushed them to the dealer in second-hand goods, disposing of the lot! Then while his astonished wife weeps and raves, he sweeps all her precious dresses into a bundle and trudges off to get the best possible price for them at the market.

Almost hysterical, she tries to warn the children to hide their things as she sees Ali returning with that mysterious look in his clever eyes. She is too late, for he grabs their things, and rushes off to sell them, too. The cow, the goats, the sheep— what few animals they have he drives off to the market. His relatives come with a perplexed look on their faces. Never have they known Ali to act in such a strange way. His poor wife wrings her hands in desperation, while all the neighbours can do is to shake their heads in wonder.

Ali returns with a furniture dealer who enters the house and appraises the value of the beds, the chairs, the table, even the empty cupboards. They agree on a price, and in a few minutes the humble cottage is emptied of everything. Not a saleable item remains among Ali's and his family's possessions!

The only smiling face visible anywhere among the family and relatives is Ali's. With a happy glint in his eye he counts the cash he has realized from these sudden, frenzied sales, and with a barely audible mutter of "I'll be back," he dashes off to see the rich landlord.

"What has got into him?" his brother asks Ali's wife.

"I can't imagine," she replies.

"When did this strange behaviour begin?" asks a neighbor.

"Well," she muses, "it began last night when he came home from ploughing in the rented field where he is trying to make a garden. He was different. I have never seen him act this way before— he hardly spoke; he hardly tasted the delicious supper I had prepared; and he barely noticed the children. And once I awoke during the night to hear him muttering in his sleep: 'The box! The box! The treasure! I caught it with my plough!' I don't know what he meant, though. He seemed delirious, so I shook him to get him out of his dream.

"He groaned, then turned over and went back to sleep. Soon he was talking in his sleep again, and this time I heard him say: 'I must buy the field! Even if it takes every coin I have!' I just don't know what to make of it all."

While the perplexed family and neighbours were still whispering among themselves outside the empty home, Ali came striding down the street with a look of triumph on his face, as though he had conquered an empire. He was waving a sheet of paper in his hands. "Look," he cried, "the title-deed! It's ours!" He swept his wife up in his arms and then, delirious with joy, he caught and hugged each of his bewildered children.

"My dear wife and children," he announced, "you think I've gone berserk, but I haven't. I am quite aware of what I have done. Don't cry for your ragged clothes I have sold, or for your cracked dishes and beat-up pots and sufurias I have hauled off to the market, dear wife and children. Don't mourn for the loss of the donkey and cart by which I earned our pitiful little income, or for the patched-up furniture that is gone. As of this moment, we are wealthy beyond our wildest dreams. ... I have bought the field!"

"What field? What do you mean?" demanded his still perplexed wife.

Then Ali gathered the little group around him to tell the story. Yesterday he had been ploughing in the hot sunshine, his weary body bathed with sweat. "Must I always toil like this," he asked himself, "and earn so little?" Then as his faithful ox pulled on the plough, he felt it strike something solid buried in the ground. It wasn't a stone; you can feel the difference between the plough striking buried wood or stone. It was wood. A wooden box!

Why should there be a box buried in the landlord's field? Ali didn't know, but as a child he had heard tales told of lucky people who had discovered buried boxes of treasure in various parts of the Middle East. Some worried rich man of ancient times would bury his gold, silver, and jewels when he heard of enemy armies marching to conquer the land. He would plan to return after the war was over and recover his wealth, for only he would know where it was hidden. But if the rich man should be lost in the war, his box would remain where he hid it.

Ali looked this way and that to be sure no one was watching, and then getting down on his hands and knees he scraped the earth away until the old treasure chest lay exposed. Carefully he opened the rotting lid, and stared in astonishment at the treasure of gold, silver, and precious stones glinting in the afternoon sunlight.

What to do? The only legal way to possess this fabulous wealth would be to own the land in which it was buried. After he had replaced the cover and carefully packed the earth over his discovery, he resumed ploughing, his mind racing in a search for some way to buy the field. The landlord had once offered to sell it to him, but Ali realized that the price demanded would take everything he possessed.

He didn't dare tell anyone of his find, not even his wife. Hence his strange behaviour when the sun rose next morning.

This true story has thrilled untold millions of people for nearly 2,000 years. It illustrates the value of true religion. The treasure hidden in the field represents a living faith in the one true Allah, without which the wealthiest person on earth is no better than a pauper. The sale of all Ali's possessions represents the sacrifice that you and I must make if we would have this precious treasure. Ali's delirious joy at possessing the field represents the happiness that forever fills our hearts as we gain these true riches.

The astonishment of Ali's family and friends represents the wonderment of our family and friends at the change that faith produces in us!

This oft-repeated tale told by Jesus (Issa, son of Mary) brings good news to every human being on earth. Your plough has already unearthed a treasure worth more than any prince's gold. And you *can* buy the field where the treasure is. Every man and woman is the lucky Ali. All he or she needs is an appreciation of the treasure—a realization of its value. Nothing that Ali did was worthy of merit in itself; he simply knew a good thing when he saw it!

This book in your hands could be more valuable to you than actually finding a box of gold in your backyard some midnight. It can give you a faith to live by. King Solomon, son of the Prophet David (Daud), who was known for his great wisdom, for a time lost his faith in God. Of this time he said:

> "Meaningless! Meaningless!" says the Teacher. "Utterly meaningless! Everything is meaningless." What does man gain from all his labor at which he toils under the sun?[1]

Fortunately, King Solomon recovered his faith in Allah. But his despair is the cup from which most people drink today.

This book is about buried treasure. It is not that Allah has hidden his "wealth," hoping we won't find it. On the contrary, it is he who is guiding the plough of our lives to strike the treasure box itself. He *wants* us to possess it.

God sent a message through an ancient prophet, Jeremiah the son of Hilkiah. These beautiful verses describe how a believer feels about this priceless spiritual treasure:

> "Let not the wise man boast of his wisdom
> Or the strong man boast of his strength
> Or the rich man boast of his riches,
> But let him who boasts boast about this:
>   That he understands and knows me,
>   That I am the Lord, who exercises kindness,
>   Justice and righteousness on earth."[2]

---

1. Ecclesiastes 1:2, 3, NIV.
2. Jeremiah 9:23, 24, NIV.

"If thou obeyest most of those on earth, they would lead thee far from Allah's way.' (*The Qur'an*, 6:117).

2
Our Tospy-Turvy World Needs True Religion

Untold millions of our fellow-men are wandering in a daze of spiritual poverty. Many realize that money and sensual pleasure do not satisfy. Except for those who do have a living faith in God, all are obsessed by fear of the future.

A little girl in school expressed her consternation at what is happening in our world:

> If I were the sun
> And I saw the things that people had done
> I would eclipse myself
> Forever.[1]

The daily horror of murders, rapes, terrorist bombings and much more, is blood-chilling; and if the sun could feel, it would indeed want to hide its face from beholding this never-ending agony. And even where there is peace (if there is such a place left on earth?), there is often starvation and poverty.

---

1. Quoted in *Pornography, the Longford Report* (Coronet), p. 347.

The world dared once to hope that World War I would be "the war to end all wars." Then the nations hoped that World War II would do the trick, but now many years after the United Nations was organized to do away with war, machine guns and bombs still shatter the security of people in almost every land. The atomic bomb in 1945 killed 87,000 people in a few seconds. Then, seven years later, came the hydrogen bomb that was a thousand times stronger. Only two years later came the cobalt bomb with radio-active clouds 300,000 times stronger than the deadly cloud resulting from the explosion of the first hydrogen bomb. Now we have the "clean" one, the neutron bomb, that will just kill the people but leave the buildings intact. It would be impossible to find more accurate words to describe the way people feel today than those spoken nearly 2,000 years ago in the Holy Injil:

> On the earth, nations will be in anguish and perplexity at the roaring and tossing of the sea. Men will faint from terror, apprehensive of what is coming on the world.[2]

You have to be blind not to see the evidence: the fabric of society is tearing itself apart like the rotten threads of an old garment. Those who believe in Allah and respect his Word are amazed and afraid as they watch the world taking a nose-dive into a new Dark Age.

What will Allah do to help the situation? Will he lead forth his armies of righteousness in a new holy war (Jihad) to set the world's wrongs right? Will a new world ruler arise somewhere on the horizon to guide the nations into conformity with Allah's holy commandments? How can the wicked be put down and the righteous be exalted to power?

Will the Super-powers be allowed to go mad and destroy each other (and the rest of the world as well) with nuclear

---

2. Luke 21:25, 26, NIV.

war or "clean" neutron bombs? Or is the world doomed to continue spending a million dollars *a minute* on sophisticated armaments? Must the great nations continue to create huge arsenals of weapons that often become obsolete before they are used, while hungry widows and children starve for the simple necessities that the money spent on these lethal weapons would easily provide?

Will the rich, luxury-accustomed nations continue to pile up treasures while the developing nations slide further back into poverty? How will the world's poor and needy ever obtain justice?

For thousands of years history has record of much suffering and atrocity, but at no other time have more innocent people had to suffer than during this bloody century:

World War I (1914-1918) unleashed a horror the world had never before dreamed of—war on a massive scale of terror and cruelty. For the first time, aeroplanes fought in the sky and bombed cities, and submarines torpedoed ships without warning. The death toll for four years of this madness came to about 10 million, casualties totalled 33 million, and the monetary cost ran up to a massive $337,000,000,000. It came near to being world suicide.

The peace that followed the end of World War I was only a momentary lull, giving the nations a chance to catch their breath before rushing into the even more horrible events of World War II (1939-1945). The advantages that peace could have brought were foolishly squandered. Again, unspeakable sorrows were thrust upon millions of people. There were nearly 16 million deaths. The monetary cost far outstripped that of World War I, reaching $1,154,000,000,000, with property damage alone amounting to $239,000,000,000.

Thoughtful, innocent people beat their breasts and cried out, "Where is Allah?"

Since nuclear war was made possible by the atomic bombs dropped on Hiroshima on August 6, 1945 and Nagasaki three days later, the entire world lives under the impending shadow of a holocaust that could wipe out civilization. Children have nightmares because of this constant dread. Since the end of World War II, the world has suffered 130 wars, in which millions more have lost their lives. The combined armed forces of Africa number more than 1,650,000, costing $9,269,000,000 a year to maintain. Africa's military spending grows at the rate of 33 per cent a year, the fastest in the world!

At the same time, the Super-powers are stockpiling sufficient nuclear weapons to wipe each other out completely. Their motivation is the fear engendered by the bitter memories of World War II, but what would either side really gain?

Meanwhile the nations of the Middle East seethe with tension and animosity. Not only war, but also the most horrible atrocities involving helpless women and children, bring sorrow to every feeling heart. Even little children have been pressed into bearing arms, and exposed to the horrors of battle. And when the wars are over, what gains have been won?

Why does a loving, compassionate Allah permit this madness to continue? Half of the world's 70 million destitute refugees are in Africa, and of all continents, Africa can least afford to feed them. The United Nations Food and Agriculture Organization estimates that the average African has 10 per cent less to eat today than 10 years ago. This is due to rapidly increasing populations and constantly falling food production.

In the meantime, millions of people have become hardened to the threats of annihilation and say, "Let us eat, drink, and be merry, for tomorrow we die." "Let us enjoy the sensual pleasures of the moment" is their philosophy, for they think they see no evidence of the intervention, or even the existence, of an almighty, compassionate, caring Allah. Hence, immorality, pornography, divorce, sensuality, alcoholism, and drug abuse are increasing alarmingly. Massive corruption rots away the foundations of business and political structures.

Says the honoured Qur'an:

> And who goes further astray than he who follows his lust in the place of guidance from Allah. Lo! Allah guides not such oppressors.[3]
> Hast thou seen him who chooses for his god his own lust? Would thou be guardian over him? Or deem thou that most of them hear or understand? They are but as the cattle—nay, but they are farther astray.[4]

The earnest, sincere efforts of many dedicated government leaders to advance the prosperity of Third World peoples are held back by the tenacious tentacles of this godless corruption.

How true are these words from the honoured Qur'an:

> There is not a nation but a warner hath passed among them.[5]
> And for every nation there is a Messenger.[6]

It doesn't take a genius to recognize that our modern world desperately needs a spiritual revival and reformation in order to avoid moral and/or physical suicide.

Millions realize that the world needs a true religion. Allah is not asleep, or uncaring. He is speaking to the hearts of men, women, and youth all over the globe. There *is* a path to salvation—Allah has not forgotten us.

A well-known Hadith says: "If Allah causes you to lead a single person on the right path, it is better for you than to possess the world with all that it contains."[7] This book is a search for that true path, where we will find answers to our questions.

---

3. *The Qur'an*, 28:50.
4. *The Qur'an*, 25:43, 44.
5. *The Qur'an*, 35:24.
6. *The Qur'an*, 10:48.
7. Quoted in *Awake to the Call of Islam*, vol. 3, no. 6, p. 5.

"Ask them, O Prophet, 'Why not the original path, the path of Ibrahim?' He was a man of faith, and not an idolater." (*The Qur'an*, 2:135).

3
Abraham's Islam

There was no worship of images in the time of Adam and Eve for them to protest against, as did the prophet Muhammad at Mecca: but idol worship was almost universal in the days of our father, Hazrat Abraham (Ibrahim), 2,400 years before Muhammad.

You can imagine what happened when Abraham was a boy. We know that his father Terah (Tarikh) shared the blindness of his day in that he worshiped idols.[1] (The "god" commonly worshiped in his home city was the moon-god). Father Terah would probably say to young Abraham, "Come, son, it's time to worship the moon-god."

"Father, I agree that the moon is beautiful, shining in nightly splendour that surpasses even the stars. I love to stand on our roof top and watch it rise in the cool of a clear evening; but why should we worship it?"

"But son, everybody does. Why not you, too?"

---

1. Joshua 24:2; the Arabic name is for Terah is Tarikh.

"Father, perhaps 'everybody' is not right. Surely there is a God who is greater than the moon, the sun, or the stars!"

"But your childhood friends all go to worship the moon-god and the other idols in the temple, and the worship is beautiful and alluring. Why do you insist on being different? Even your brothers Haran and Nahor worship the idols."

"Yes, I am sure there are pleasures in this idolatrous worship, but Allah, who has created all things in heaven and earth, has spoken to my heart, and I am willing to be different from everybody else by worshiping him alone!"

It was as if Abraham boldly proclaimed, *La Ilaha illa I' Lah* (There is no god but God). As Kenneth Oster wisely says, "Monotheism is a high mountain that must be scaled, not a valley into which man naturally slithers. ... Monotheism ... is a revealed truth, not the outcropping of any man's private cogitations. ... The natural man slides into polytheism, ... the result of man's naturally sinful inclinations."[2]

Abraham was different, and the whole world can praise Allah that he found a youth willing to stand alone for the truth. How dark would have been this world had it not been for Abraham's shining example of loyalty to the one true God! With the exception of his faith, there was darkness everywhere.

Abraham saw a light that others in his home city did not see. While he was still young, he witnessed to the truth and proved to his family and the people of his city that idols cannot speak, and are worthless. Some people accepted his witness; but Abraham was the pioneer. The Lord gave him strength to be loyal and to stand alone.

As a boy, Abraham grew up in the great city of Ur. His father was wealthy. The cuneiform texts on numerous clay

---

2. Kenneth Oster, *Islam Reconsidered, A brief historical background to the religion and thought of the Moslem world*, pp. 29-31.

tablets dug up in Ur tell us of the high state of education and civilization in Abraham's home city during his time. As a boy, Abraham attended schools where he learned reading, writing, arithmetic, and geography. We know this because many school exercises written on clay tablets have been recovered from the buried ruins of ancient Ur.

Abraham's father's house was doubtless a good one, much like the handsome, two-storey brick houses excavated at Ur. It would have been well constructed, with a central courtyard, and inside plumbing connected to a city sewage system. In fact his home was even more modern and comfortable than some cities in the same area can boast of today, after nearly 3,800 years! The idea that Abraham was a simple, uneducated poor nomad is wrong. Allah gave him great wisdom and wealth. He was highly respected.

Although his father never gave up the worship of idols completely, he was impressed by his son's faith and holy boldness. He joined Abraham in responding to the call of Allah to leave Ur and start out for the land that would be shown them. They were to shine as candles in the night and preserve the knowledge and worship of the true Allah in the polytheistic world around them.

Abraham's father and his family went with him as far as the town of Haran. There they all settled down until Terah died. Most were half-and-half worshippers of Allah, influenced by young Abraham's monotheism, but still unwilling to be "different" enough to worship Allah *alone*. Nahor's grandson, Laban, still had idols in his home many years later, for we read that Rachel, Jacob's wife, stole them from him.[3]

When Terah finally died, Abraham, now 75 years of age, again heard the voice of Allah calling him to move on to a

---

3. Genesis 31:19.

new country. His brother Nahor did not have the faith and courage of Abraham and stayed behind. We can imagine the two brothers saying good-bye.

"Come, brother Nahor, for I have heard the voice of Allah calling."

"What does he say, brother Abraham?"

"He has said, 'Leave your native land, your relatives, and your father's home, and go to a country that I am going to show you. I will give you many descendants, and you will become a great nation. I will bless you and make your name famous, so that you will be a blessing. ... And through you I will bless all the nations.'[4] Come, brother Nahor, and share these blessings with me!"

"No, brother Abraham, I don't have the faith and courage to be different that you have. I am too weak. Let me stay and become part of the crowd of my friends and relatives that live here. Besides, the lush grazing lands of Haran promise more wealth than I can see in the unknown land you speak of."

So Nahor stayed behind, and several of his grand-daughters became the wives of Abraham's descendants. But Abraham became truly "famous" in all the world, and "the father of many nations."[5] Hundreds of millions of people claim him as their "father" today—including millions who cannot claim mere physical descent. Allah honours and sustains anyone who steps out alone to follow truth!

Think of Allah on his throne in heaven, merciful and compassionate to the sons of men. But when men worship idols, or turn their backs on him, he is deeply hurt by such insults. He longs for someone to represent him among men; to be a witness to his power and compassion. When Abraham was willing to be his representative among men, Allah was

---

4. Genesis 12:1, NIV.
5. Genesis 17:5.

delighted with his servant. He said of Abraham, "I know him, that he will command his children and his household after him, and they shall keep the way of the Lord, to do justice and judgment; that the Lord may bring upon Abraham that which he hath spoken of him."[6]

In other words, Allah trusted Abraham like you trust a friend whom you know. Allah and this man became friends! Allah in heaven stooped low enough to be a Companion to a man on earth. When his "friend" Abraham prayed to him, Allah was pleased to hear and answer him. Abraham was his friend. He had formed a special relationship with him, and from then on the world was to be different.

Allah's part in this special relationship was to love Abraham in a unique way, as we shall see; Abraham's part was to respond to this love that came from heaven. He valued this close friendship with Allah even more than his beautiful brick home in Ur, and the companionship of his family and relatives at Haran with its lush pastures.

The word "Muslim" (from *aslama*) means one who is completely submitted to Allah. The reason for such submission is not the fear that Allah will beat you if you don't submit, but it is a deep heart-respect for his character of righteousness and unselfish love. He says: "Heaven is my throne and the earth is my footstool. ... [But] this is the one I esteem: he who is humble and contrite in spirit, and trembles at my word."[7]

Such "trembling" is not that of a cowering slave who fears his master's lash if he does not bow before him. The prophet Isaiah is speaking of the thrill, the shivers of awe and delight that go up and down one's spine as he contemplates the majesty and glory of Allah's love. This is worship. Animals can never know such a delightful thrill; neither can brutish

---

6. Genesis 18:19.
7. Isaiah 66:1, 2, NIV.

people who keep their eyes only on the deceitful pleasures and riches of this wicked world. They live or exist in a state of death, wisely spoken of as being "dead in trespasses and sins."[8] But the one who is truly submitted to Allah has begun a new life, even that which is eternal. He is truly a Muslim.

Abraham deserves that honourable title!

Now let us go with him as he takes his long journey across the desert to a land that he has never seen, following the call of Allah.

By faith we accompany Abraham through the written Word of the Holy Scriptures. They are an honest, reliable account of Abraham's witness for Allah, who promised him that "through you I will bless all nations." How could Allah "bless all the nations" unless he preserved a pure and true record of his promises through his Holy Word?

Allah inspired the prophet Moses (Musa) to write a faithful account of Abraham's devotion. He called Abraham to be "the father of many nations," one through whom he said: "I will bless all the nations." Allah also inspired the preservation of Moses' record. Thus Moses' words were not for Israel alone but for all the world, because all who have true faith in Allah would claim Abraham as their "father."

The Old Testament Scriptures are the most accurately preserved books that have survived from those ancient times. The accidental discovery by Bedouins (1947) of the famous Dead Sea Scrolls has provided the world with authentic documents which are dated by experts as having been copied as early as the 2nd century B.C. All of the documents found in the Dead Sea caves date from before A.D. 70. Some experts even say that the document of Leviticus dates from the 5th or 4th century B.C. the amazing thing is that these ancient documents are found to be almost *word for word* identical to the

---

8. Ephesians 2:1.

Old Testament Scriptures used today, the only variants being slight differences in spelling, such as Abraham or Ibrahim. Everyone knows it is the same name. Even these minor variants prove the faithful transmission of the sacred text![9]

The one who believes the Word of Allah may rejoice in the confidence that he has preserved his glorious truth throughout the ages.

No other written records from the ancient times of Abraham or Moses or the prophets give evidence of divine inspiration as do the Holy Scriptures. All other ancient documents or inscriptions tend to vanity, to fulsome praise of weak, mortal men. The Holy Scriptures faithfully recount the mistakes and failures of even great men, that the glory and honour may go only to Allah himself, who alone deserves praise. The unmistakable heartbeat of inspiration pulses through the Scriptures. In simple yet grand language, the heavenly concepts are expressed.

Thus it is with confidence that we can take our journey by faith with the honoured prophet Abraham, and recapture the essence of his Islam!

---

9. Incidentally, the New Testament Scriptures have also been confirmed by the discovery at Faiyum in Egypt of documents that scholars agree date to the time of the Roman emperor Trajan (A.D. 98-117), only a short time after the death of the apostle John himself. One of these documents contains a portion of John's Gospel, demonstrating that its text is confirmed as correct by the discovery of this ancient fragment. This shows how that Gospel was in circulation in Egypt at that early time. Clear evidence, going back centuries before the time of the Prophet Muhammad, shows that the Gospels and other New Testament books have not been altered. Differences in the ancient manuscripts are only minor variants of spelling or syntax, as is the case with the Old Testament manuscripts. The message comes through intact.

The Holy Scriptures speak to the heart of mankind. Their power to change human hearts, and to speak peace to the mind and soul, is their credential of divine authority.

"Say, Verily my Lord hath directed me into a right way, a true religion, the sect of Abraham the orthodox; and he was no idolater." (*The Qur'an*, 6:163).

4

Abraham's Faith Astonishes the World

In Hazrat Abraham's day it was not the done thing to leave your parents' home and strike off on your own to some distant country a thousand kilometres away. Especially was this true if you had no land, or prospect of buying land, in the area where you were going. Imagine that no one has invited you except Allah, and of course you have never seen him, for he is invisible. You are burning all your bridges behind you, and if things go wrong in your new country of adoption, you cannot return from whence you came. This is how it was with the prophet Abraham. What magnificent confidence he had in the unseen Allah!

Allah calls men and women today, just as he called Abraham long ago, and he is still the faithful Guide to all who believe his promise. Abraham is "the father of all them that believe,"[1] and all who have true faith will likewise be ready to sacrifice everything earthly in order to follow his call.

---

1. Romans 4:11.

After Abraham's and Sarah's long journey, they were tempted to wonder if Allah had forsaken them, for when they arrived in the land of Canaan they found that there was a "grievous famine" there. A person without faith would have turned around and gone back home again to Haran, but not Abraham. He went still further, searching for food, all the way to Egypt.[2] Infidels sometimes blaspheme Allah, saying that he should have provided food for his faithful, hungry servant in Canaan, whence he had called him to go. But Abraham's faith did not falter. Allah was teaching us through Abraham's experience that trials and hardships come even to faithful believers, and that he will never forsake us. The whole world has been moved by the sight of this lonely pilgrim wandering through strange lands in answer to God's call.

Later he returned to Bethel "unto the place where his tent had been at the beginning."[3] All around him were idolaters, yet in every place where he pitched his tent he erected an altar and "called on the name of the Lord."[4] Allah rewarded his faith, for there were always some Canaanites who watched, wondered, listened, and joined him in the worship of Allah.

Abraham's faith was again severely tried when there was not enough pasture land for both his flocks and those of his nephew Lot (Lut). He said to Lot: "Choose any part of the land you want. You go one way, and I'll go the other."[5] Lot selfishly chose "for himself" the "whole Jordan Valley, all the way to Zoar," which was "like the Garden of the Lord." That left the poorer land to Abraham. "Lot ... camped near Sodom, whose people were wicked and sinned against the Lord."[6] Soon he and his family became entangled in wicked city life and only Allah's compassion later saved him.

---

2. Genesis 12:10-12.
3. Genesis 13:3, 4.
4. Genesis 13:4.
5. Genesis 13:8, 9, TEV.
6. Genesis 13:10-13, TEV.

Meanwhile, Allah comforted his "friend" Abraham: "From where you are, look carefully in all directions. I am going to give you and your descendants all the land that you see, and it will be yours forever."⁷ North, east, south, west—there was no limit to the promise!

Lot later lost everything he possessed, including his sons, in the fiery destruction of Sodom. Although Allah had promised to give all the land to Abraham, he had unselfishly parted with the best of it. Why was he so willing to give up worldly property and to keep on living only in a tent? Is it possible that he saw some deeper blessing in the divine promise than we see on the surface?

Look again at the promise Allah made to Abraham: "*All the land*" that he could see was to be his and his descendants' "for ever." This included far more than Canaan or Palestine, for the promise included the whole earth as an everlasting possession.⁸ "Blessed are the meek," says Jesus (el-Mesih Issa ben Maryam), "for they shall inherit the *earth*."⁹ Hazrat Abraham is the "father of all them that believe," and his true "descendants" are "the meek." All "who also walk in the steps of that *faith* of our father Abraham," "who is the father of us all,"¹⁰ will inherit the "land promised to Abraham.

The compassionate, merciful Allah is too kind to expect His servants, the faithful descendants of Abraham, to be content to live forever in slums, hovels, and deserts, or camp under the threatening stare of machine guns. This present earth is not their "home." There is something better for them in Allah's plan. The "earth" that the "meek" are to inherit will not be this ruined, war-ravaged, and often filthy place that we know now. It will be a "new earth … which," says Allah,

---

7. Genesis 13:15.
8. Genesis 17:8, TEV.
9. Matthew 5:5.
10. Romans 4:12, 16.

"I create."[11] And those who live there will indeed possess it forever, for He says: "My people ... will fully enjoy the things that they have worked for. ... I will bless them and their descendants for all time to come. ... There will be nothing harmful or evil."[12]

This "new earth" is the Paradise described in the honoured Qur'an as the land "watered by rivers; its food is perpetual, and its shade also: this shall be the reward of those who fear God."[13]

It is plain for anyone to see that this is the only possible understanding of Allah's promise, for Abraham in his lifetime hardly owned a square metre of land in Canaan at any time. In fact, he was obliged to buy a little place where he might bury his dead wife—the Cave of Machpelah. (The mosque of Haram now covers the site.) Either Allah told Abraham a lie (which is unthinkable), or the promise is to be fulfilled in the *new* earth that He shall re-create.

The prophet David (Daud), whose psalms are among the most beautiful poetry in the world, composed this hymn of assurance:

> Soon the wicked will disappear;
> you may look for them, but you won't find them;
> the humble will possess the land
> and enjoy prosperity and peace. ...
>
> The descendants of the wicked will be driven out.
> The righteous will possess the land
> and live in it forever.[14]

What King David understood is that neither Abraham nor any of us has as yet received the promised inheritance. It will come at the last day! The people of Jerusalem once thought that

---

11. Isaiah 65:17, 18.
12. Isaiah 65:22-25, TEV.
13. *The Qur'an*, 13:35.
14. Psalm 37:10, 11, 28, 29, TEV.

their city was the inheritance of Abraham and his descendants, but they were the ones who united in a terrible plan to kill the Christ. Later they martyred one of his followers, named Stephen. His dying speech mentioned Abraham. He said that Allah "did not then give Abraham any part of it [this land] as his own, not even a square metre of ground."[15] Thus the martyr Stephen denied that Jerusalem was Abraham's city. He looked forward in faith to the resurrection day.

The first generation of those who followed Jesus accepted the *Letter to the Hebrews* as sent to them under God's inspiration. In this letter Hazrat Abraham is mentioned as an example to us all:

> It was faith that made Abraham obey when God called him to go out to a country which God had promised to give him. He left his own country without knowing where he was going. By faith he lived as a foreigner in the country that God had promised him. He lived in tents. ... For Abraham was waiting for the city which God has designed and built, the city with permanent foundations. ...
> These persons ... did not receive the things God had promised, but from a long way off they saw them and welcomed them, and admitted openly that they were foreigners and refugees on earth. Those who say such things make it clear that they are looking for a country of their own. ... It was a better country they longed for, the heavenly country. And so God is not ashamed for them to call him their God, because he has prepared a city for them.[16]

Is it foolish to have this "faith of Abraham," this supreme concern for the *eternal* blessings? Such faith is what has provided all the true blessings the world has ever enjoyed! True and lasting temporal prosperity is a by-product of that spiritual faith.

---

15. Acts 7:5, 6, TEV.
16. Hebrews 11:8-16, TEV.

Unbelievers forget the *true* promise that God made to Abraham, and demand the shell, despising the sweet fruit within. They want this earth's things *now*, determined even to create envy, strife, and murder to get them. They destroy their own peace and happiness, and that of their children, never finding anything on earth that they can truly hold secure. They cannot even sleep at night for fear of losing what they do have.

True believers, however, understand the promise of Allah exactly as did Abraham—it includes Paradise; but for now, they are content to worship Allah as "foreigners and refugees on earth," knowing that he has "prepared a city for them." They know true peace, even as Abraham did.

For the remainder of his life Abraham had to live in a tent. His lovely, two-storey brick home back in Ur was a thing of the past. He had to live far from the pleasant civilization he had known. He was a strange kind of pioneer, for he built no house for himself anywhere.

The Holy Book says that Abraham and Sarah died "in faith," and were buried in that little plot at Machpelah for which they had paid hard money. When Sarah died, he "left the place where his wife's body was lying, went to the Hittites, and said, 'I am a foreigner living here among you; sell me some land, so that I can bury my wife.'" Think of it! Allah had promised him all the land he could see, north, east, south, and west, even the whole earth; yet here he is begging to buy a tiny cave "so that I can own it as a burial ground"![17]

If you had asked Abraham at this time, "Where is the evidence that Allah has kept his promise to you?" I'm sure he would have responded with: "I am a foreigner and refugee on this earth. It is a better country I long for—the heavenly

---

17. Genesis 23:3-9.

one. I will not be satisfied to take the shell of the fruit and leave the kernel. Life on this earth is full of troubles—see, there lies the body of my faithful wife Sarah. This *earth* is not what Allah has promised me. He has promised me something better. My faith in him has sustained me all these years and provided meaning for life, enriching my life with more peace and happiness than if I had owned all of Mesopotamia! It is better to follow Allah as a "foreigner and refugee" than to sit on a throne of gold in a selfish world."

Abraham has two kinds of "descendants": those who are his literal genetic descendants, and those who "walk in the steps of that *faith* of our father Abraham." When Allah called him to leave his "native land ... and go to a land that I am going to show you," he added something more precious than all the gold and silver in the whole world: "You will be a blessing, ... and through you I will bless *all* the nations."[18] This included a greater joy than merely inheriting Paradise, for it meant that the world's salvation should come through his descendants. Such spiritual joy is greater than mere physical or sensual pleasure.

Another most important truth is that there is something which is vitally necessary for Abraham and his descendants to have in order for them to inherit Paradise as an everlasting possession. The holy apostle Peter declares that "in keeping with his [Allah's] promise we are looking forward to a new heaven and a new earth, the home of righteousness."[19] This means that Allah included the blessed gift of righteousness, in his promise to Abraham. Only this righteousness could make him and his descendants fit to inherit such a Paradise.

Man does not naturally possess that righteousness, any more than he naturally possesses that "new earth." It is the

---

18. Genesis 12:2, 3, TEV, emphasis supplied.
19. 2 Peter 3:13, NIV.

gift of Allah's grace. It is on the basis of Abraham's faith that Allah can do this for him and for his true descendants who "walk in the steps of that faith of our father Abraham." What glorious depths of meaning are included in Allah's promises, things that lie far deeper than a superficial glance reveals!

Abraham has already blessed "all nations" with his faith, his knowledge of the truth of Allah, and his heart-appreciation of Allah's glorious character. His faith was a connection between heaven and earth, the vital life-line that would save the world from the self-destruction which follows idolatry and selfishness.

Abraham's true "children," therefore, are those who have his faith, regardless of the national, racial, or colour group from which they may come. Are you willing to be one of his true "descendants"?

"Lo, those of mankind who have the best claim to Abraham are those who followed him." (*The Qur'an*, 3:68)

5

How Abraham Became "The Friend of God"

The kings of Sodom and Gomorrah got tangled up in a war which went against them, and their enemy captured everything, including their food. Lot, Abraham's nephew (Lut), "was living in Sodom, so they took him and all his possessions."[1] It was Allah's merciful way of warning Lot to get out of that wicked place!

When Abraham heard what had happened, he called 318 men from his camp to go with him to rescue Lot. The little "army" marched nearly 400 kilometres, "attacked the enemy by night, and defeated them, ... and recovered [got back] all the loot that had been taken. He also brought back his nephew Lot and his possessions."[2]

"Keep the loot, but give me back all my people," the king of Sodom pleaded, but Abraham, still looking for a heavenly city rather than earthly riches, replied: "I will not keep anything of yours, not even a thread or a sandal strap ... I will

---

1. Genesis 14:12, TEV.
2. Genesis 14:14-16, TEV.

take nothing for myself."³ But the servant of God did give a tenth of all as "tithe" to the Lord's priest, Melchizedek.⁴

Now we find Allah again speaking to his "friend": "I will shield you from danger and give you a great reward."⁵

In spite of this something troubled Abraham. He wasn't worried about those heathen kings coming back to get revenge on him, but how about Allah's promise to give him "many descendants"? Allah had raised his expectations sky high with this promise when he left Ur, but to date not even baby number one had arrived. Had God forsaken his faithful servant? Or worse yet, had he deceived him?

This wonderful promise was ringing in Abraham's ears night and day, but why didn't Allah *do* something to fulfil it?

Finally, Abraham decided that he expected *him* to do something. He thought of a plan! Perhaps he was trusting Allah too much, for Sarah had not become a mother. Abraham decided that *he* must do the actual work of fulfilling the divine promise to him.

Therefore he made a plan to adopt his servant Eliezer of Damascus as his legal heir. Through *him* he would have those "many descendants". It was common custom in old Mesopotamia for wealthy but childless couples to adopt a favourite slave as heir to all their property. He would then care for them in their old age. After all, Eliezer had been born

---

3. Genesis 14:21-24, TEV.

4. Everyone who has the faith of Abraham will also return to Allah one-tenth of all that heaven gives him as "increase." By doing so Abraham confessed his faith that Allah was the source of all that he possessed. Returning a faithful tenth to Allah is his appointed way for us to say "thank you" for all the gifts of life which we enjoy. The prophet Malachi says that withholding the tithe is robbing God, and calls on us to "prove him" by returning to him a faithful tenth or tithe; then we can watch him keep his promise to "open to you the windows of heaven, and pour you out a blessing, that there shall not be room enough to receive it" (Malachi 3:8-10).

5. Genesis 15:1, TEV.

in Abraham's own house. Perhaps that is what Allah had all along intended him to do! This was the only plan the aged patriarch could think of.

No, not at all, Allah said. "This slave Eliezer will *not* inherit your property; your own son will be your heir."[6]

Abraham was astonished! There was no gynaecologist available to cure Sarah of her infertility, and besides, she was now too old to conceive a baby. Abraham could see no way for this astounding promise ever to be fulfilled. Try to put yourself in his place. What an impasse!

Abraham tossed and turned on his bed that night and racked his brain, but he could see no solution to the problem. The cool desert breeze flapped the tent awning as Abraham lay awake in the darkness pondering this amazing new revelation. "*Your own son* … !" He had no son, and Sarah was well past the time of child-bearing. "*Your own son* …!" Oh, how Abraham had often yearned for a boy whom he could call "my son," but the older he became, the less it seemed that Allah's promise of "many descendants" would be fulfilled. He was willing to love Eliezer as a son, and Eliezer's children as grandchildren, but no, Allah had said that he would not accept such a plan of Abraham's own devising.

Suddenly Abraham heard the divine voice invite him to come outside the tent. Not a cloud speckled the depths of the moonless night. Millions of sparkling stars twinkled in the crystal clear mountain air while the gentle breeze caressed his upturned face. "Look at the sky and try to count the stars," Allah commanded.

Abraham doubtless had much better eyesight than we have these days. Sometimes what we see as one star turns out, through the giant modern telescopes, to be a galaxy composed

---

6. Isaiah 65:17, 18.

of unnumbered stars. The Milky Way, for example, is made up of 100 thousand million stars similar to our own sun.[7] Some scientists believe that stars known as quasars are really far distant galaxies like the Milky Way. Stars, suns, shining galaxies—the night sky was glittering with these untold billions of heavenly bodies. Abraham could not even begin to count them, even if he had had a modern computer at his disposal.

"You will have as many descendants as that," said Allah.

Ah, thought Abraham, not only is the great promise renewed; now it is multiplied beyond my happiest dreams! Again he explored the heavens with his eyes. Allah waited for him to respond. They were friends, remember, he and Abraham. Would Abraham reject the promise? Would he angrily accuse Allah of deceiving him with news that was too good to be true? So many unbelievers and infidels have reacted that way, rebelling against his great love and compassion.

Eliezer is not to be one of those stars; "*your own son ... ,*" a baby boy yet unknown and unseen, will be the progenitor of those myriads of descendants. Is it too much to believe?

A thousand volts of electricity may be ready to flow through a wire, but unless we complete the circuit by switching the power on, nothing happens. God has already taught his "friend" that his own "works," like adopting Eliezer, will not bring about the fulfilment of the divine promise. God alone must do the work; but how is Abraham to turn the switch so that the power in the divine promise becomes effective? Allah cannot force all these "descendants" on Abraham if he should be unwilling to accept and believe the promise, for he is merciful and compassionate and will not abuse or misuse his faithful servant. Abraham is his "friend," and no one will force a friend against his own will. How will Abraham respond?

---

7. *World Book Encyclopedia*, vol. 18, p. 474.

Abraham reviews the years of disappointment through which he has suffered. How many times has he been tempted to give up, and renounce his confidence in Allah's unfulfilled promise! Where has Allah been all these years? Why has he apparently forgotten his friend? Now he has spoken again, inviting Abraham to try to count those innumerable twinkling stars above his head, saying, "you will have as many descendants as that." "Oh, does he love me *that* much?" cries the chastened patriarch.

Tears start to trickle from Hazrat Abraham's uplifted eyes. The shining stars are swimming in his tear-brimming vision. His body begins to heave as he sobs. Oh, the mercy and love of the faithful Allah! He has not forgotten to be gracious! This tender love overwhelms Abraham, and with all his heart he responds to God's promise: "*And he believed in the Lord.*"[8] All the faith of Abraham's heart hoarded up for decades is poured out in that confession, "*I believe*." The doubts that have been warring against God are vanquished now; the fears that God is not faithful are over. Abraham's heart is now pulsating in beautiful harmony with the heart of God, and there is sweet peace between Allah and his friend. (That same peace is what *we* want!)

Let us note that Abraham made no promises to Allah. All he did was to "believe." He repented of his wrong plans to "work" that fulfilment of the promise by adopting Eliezer; nothing that he could *do* would fulfil the promise. He must *let Allah do it*! Now he appreciates not only that Allah is able to do it, but also that he is *willing* to do it. His faith is a heart-appreciation of God's character of tender love and faithfulness. It is easier for us to believe in His infinite power than in His infinite love!

---

8. Genesis 15:6

The Hebrew word used here for "believe" is the root of our word "amen," as it is also in Arabic. All Abraham could do was to cry out in the night stillness, "Amen! Amen! So be it." He placed his will, his heart-appreciation, on the side of God, and this was the faith that God was waiting for. It closed the circuit, allowing heaven's "thousand volts" of omnipotent power to flow. Allah was delighted with his servant. This was all he asked from Abraham!

Nearly 1,800 years later another father also pleased him. The story is in the Holy Injil. This father already had a son, but he had lost him, because the poor boy was possessed of a demon. "If thou canst do anything," he cries out to Jesus, "have compassion on us and help us."

Jesus directs the doubting father's "if" right back at him: "*If thou canst believe, all things are possible to him that believeth.*"

Again, as in the story of Abraham, the tears flowed from a father's eyes: "And straightway the father of the child cried out, and said with tears, Lord, I believe; help thou mine unbelief."[9] Such faith is all that Allah has ever asked from anyone; then his miracle-working power can go to work. The works are his; the faith is ours, a gift from him for us to develop and strengthen by use.

Outside his tent that brilliant starlit night, Abraham "believed in the Lord; and he [Allah] counted it [his faith] to him for righteousness."[10] The word "righteousness" means to be put right with God, to be justified. All of Abraham's doubts needed to be put right. Also his attempt to do Allah's work for him—this was something that Abraham had to learn to understand more clearly. We read in the Qur'an of how his faith grew: "Remember when Abraham said, O Lord, make this land a place of security; and grant that I and my

---

9. Mark 9:22-24, emphasis supplied.
10. Genesis 15:6.

children may avoid the worship of idols; for they, O Lord, have seduced a great number of men. ... O Lord, grant that I may be an observer of prayer, and a part of my posterity also, O Lord receive my supplication. O Lord forgive me, and my parents, and the faithful, on the day whereon an account shall be taken."[11]

When Allah counted his faith to him for righteousness, he was being put right with God. Nothing that Abraham could do could put him right with Allah. Man cannot save himself. Man cannot change his own heart. All his promises "to be good!" are worthless, for we humans are notorious for our failure to keep our promises. No human being can get himself out of the pit into which man has fallen. Modern man has discovered many amazing technological wonders, but the world's heavy burden of sadness remains: he cannot make himself good. Only Allah can do that for him, and man's faith is necessary in order to *let* him do it.

It is not enough to be told that we must be good. If it is up to us to make ourselves pure before we can come to Allah, there is no hope for us, for no man or woman can make himself or herself pure. Evil, impure thoughts and imaginings come into our hearts uninvited; feelings of hatred or resentment well up within us like brackish water bubbling out of a poisonous desert spring. For us to imagine that we have the power within ourselves to cleanse and purify that inner fountain is vain, and is the worst kind of idol-worship, for it is the worship of ourselves in place of Allah. The fountain of our hearts must be cleansed, and only Allah as a Saviour can accomplish that work.

Abraham's experience demonstrates, for all men to see plainly, that righteousness comes only by faith. By faith man is declared right; by faith he is made right.

Noah (Nuhu) is another example of a man put right by faith. Allah warned him of the coming flood. Long before the

---

11. The Qur'an, 14:35, 36, 40, 41

time of Abraham, Noah worshiped the true God, believed his holy word, and forthwith proceeded to act upon his faith. He "prepared an ark to the saving of his house; by the which he condemned the world, and became heir of the righteousness which is by faith."[12] In other words, Noah could not take praise to himself; all praise went to Allah. It was not Noah that did the good work, it was faith working in him.

Every pagan religion in the world denies this godly truth, declaring that man can save himself by his own works. Thus man's attention is diverted away from the one true object of his worship, Allah, and is placed upon himself, weak and sinful as he is. True religion turns our attention away from everybody and everything, all material objects, and directs us to look to Allah alone. This was the true faith that Abraham pioneered, and which was to be given to a world that was weary of worshiping idols.

Since faith is to be directed *alone* to Allah, it must not be directed toward man himself. Abraham denounced the senseless idol worship in Ur. But just suppose man makes an idol of himself? Is that not the worst kind of idol worship?

Suppose a man makes an idol of the good deeds he has done, the alms he has disbursed, the mosques he has built, the pilgrimages he has made, or even the prayers he has recited. It is all in vain! Idol worship is trusting the idol for righteousness and peace of heart. Suppose one trusts his own good deeds the same way? This is the most clever idolatry that Iblis has ever invented! It leads people to worship themselves, while they are deceived into thinking they are worshipping Allah! This is the essence of the idolatry that true believers protest against.

If Hazrat Abraham had made Eliezer his heir and thus fulfilled Allah's promise, Abraham would ever afterward have been a proud man, holy in his own eyes, congratulating himself

---

12. Hebrews 11:7.

on his wisdom and superior goodness. This would have led him right back into the same idolatry that he forsook in Ur, only the image he would bow to would have been himself!

Abraham would kiss no idol, no stone, no object, nor would he bow to the heavenly bodies or to himself—this is the lesson he learned that quiet starlit night. God accepted his faith for righteousness. This faith was a complete confidence in what Allah alone would do, not in what he himself could do.

The wise Maulana Sayyid Abul A'la Maududi says:

> Hazrat Ibrahim [Abraham] was born in the home of an idolater, but he came to know God and obeyed him. That is why God made him Imam of the whole world.[13]

Choose this faith of Abraham for yourself! Let Allah also be as delighted with you as he was with Abraham and let him also call you his "friend." This is what it means to be a descendant of Abraham.

---

13. *Fundamentals of Islam, Essence of Islam*, book 1, p. 8.

"Then Satan whispered to them that he might manifest unto them that which was hidden from them of their shame, and he said: Your Lord forbade you from this tree only lest ye should become angels or become one of the immortals. And he swore unto them (saying): Lo! I am a sincere adviser unto you."

"And their Lord called unto them, saying, did I not forbid you from that tree and tell you: Lo! Satan is an open enemy to you?"

(*The Qur'an*, 7:20-22).

6

Good News: Allah Shows a Smiling Face!

True religion is the only salvation for the world. All idol worship, including the worship of one's self or one's own achievements, is degrading. This degradation leads to suffering and ruin, which is contrary to Allah's loving will for the world that he created.

He is so merciful that he even cares for the needs of the animals and birds. "The eyes of all wait upon thee; and thou givest them their meat in due season. Thou openest thine hand, and satisfies the desire of every living thing."[1] "Look at the birds flying around: they do not sow seeds, gather a harvest and put it in barns; yet your Father in heaven takes care of them! Aren't you worth much more than birds?"[2] If He cares for all animals and birds alike, without arbitrary preference, how much more does He care about human beings!

Birds and animals are not evil-minded. They do not fight wars or practise genocide. Man is not an evolved animal, as

---

1. Psalm 145:15, 16.
2. Matthew 6:26, TEV.

evolutionists claim. Man was created in the image of Allah and Adam was called "the son" of Allah, because he created him noble, upright and pure, for "in the image of God created he him."[3]

Man, however, has a problem. Something has happened to him, and he is no longer noble, upright, and pure. Any daily newspaper, or newscast on radio and TV, will give us ample evidence that evil has invaded the heart and mind of mankind all over the world.

Education is powerless to make him good. Technology has only intensified his evil, and even electronics have made war all that more horrible. Higher education and wealth have succeeded only in revealing more clearly that man is selfish. Only pure, true religion will uplift and redeem him; and Abraham our "father" learned that true religion.

Brilliant sunshine is not a thousandth part as bright as is this revelation of Allah's love. Imagine a room so dark that you cannot see a sheet of white paper held before your eyes; then light a single little candle, and lo, the darkness flees! Light is always stronger than darkness. The Injil says: "The light shines in the darkness, but the darkness has not overcome it."[4]

Likewise follows the amazing truth that *love is stronger than hatred*. A little candle of Allah's love shining in one human heart will dispel darkness from an entire village. An enemy that our machine guns, poison, and bombs cannot eliminate can be changed into a friend by love, and thus the enemy is no more. This is true conquest! Love is actually the strongest force in the entire world!

The world press reported that the war between Iran and Iraq, cost Iraq one and a half thousand million dollars a month! Just think of how much money love could save these governments!

---

3. Luke 3:28; Genesis 1:27.
4. John 1:5, NIV, (marginal reading).

Love is not a human invention. No pagan idolater could ever create it. World history has given ample proof that love is something that descends to earth from above, not vice versa.

Someone may say, "Well, isn't love naturally born in the heart of mankind? Doesn't a mother love her baby whether she is a believer or a pagan? And don't husbands love their wives with physical love whether they worship Allah or not?" Yes, there are such evidences of human love; and to be fair, when we ask that question we must also note that the animals seem to have some of the same "love." A mother monkey fiercely loves her baby and will give her life for it, and such is the case with almost all animals. Is this kind of love "the Light that shines in the darkness" of the world?

No, the love that enlightens and saves the world is entirely different. There is more than one kind of love. Here is where Hazrat Abraham's faith becomes a guide enabling us to see where the two paths of love diverge. It is impossible to understand the true love of Allah unless these differences are recognized:

1. *Natural human love is possessed by the pagans and godless people as well as by those who worship God.* This natural possession includes the love of parents for their children, the love of children for their parents, and physical love. This love is earthly in its origin while the love of Allah is heavenly; it is from above. It is not natural to anyone, for it is a gift from heaven. Man can obtain it only through faith. Education or culture alone can never impart it, and man's age-long cleverness could never invent it.

2. *Natural human love is dependent on the beauty or goodness of its object.* When a man wants to marry a wife, he seeks someone who is pleasant, good, and beautiful. He is never attracted by an evil, ugly woman. Likewise, it is good people that we are drawn to for friendship and we tend to shun bad people. In contrast, Allah's love does not depend on the beauty or goodness of its object. "He makes his sun to shine on bad and

good people alike, and gives rain to those who do good and to those who do evil. Why should God reward you if you love only the people who love you? ... And if you speak only to your friends, have you done anything out of the ordinary? Even the pagans do that! You must be perfect—just as your Father in heaven is perfect."[5]

The holy record of Allah's dealings with man for thousands of years has shown that his love is not dependent on man's worthiness. Allah is greater than ourselves?

3. *Natural human love thinks of "God" as hiding from man, so that man must go in search of him.* All heathen or pagan religions are based on this fundamental idea—hence the rise of polytheism and idolatry among all primitive races and cultures the world around. Only a few very clever and persevering people are considered successful enough to "find" him. They are praised by men for their cleverness and supposed holiness.

In contrast, the true love of Allah reveals him not as hiding himself from mankind, but revealing himself to us. He has done this through his prophets through the ages. Allah himself is the Good Shepherd who goes in search of his lost sheep. He does not wait for the lost sheep to seek him out:

> "Suppose one of you has a hundred sheep and loses one of them—what does he do? He leaves the other ninety-nine sheep in the pasture and goes looking for the one that got lost until he finds it. When he finds it, he is so happy that he puts it on his shoulders and carries it back home. Then he calls he friends and neighbours together and says to them, 'I am so happy I found my lost sheep. Let us celebrate!' In the same way, I tell you, there will be more joy in heaven over one sinner who repents than over ninety-nine respectable people who do not need to repent."[6] (There is irony in those words: such "respectable" people only think they don't need to repent!)

---

5. Matthew 5:45-48, TEV.
6. Luke 15:4-7, TEV.

Allah is not hiding himself in some pagan shrine, or at Rome, or in a Buddhist temple, or at Mecca or Medina. He is not waiting for us to make an expensive and dangerous journey to seek him in his hideaway. He "is come to seek and to save that which was lost."[7] His love is active, not passive. There is a reason why this truth is so important:

If he hides himself so that man must seek him out, then man becomes the more clever of the two. Man's persistence becomes greater than Allah's ability to hide himself. This would make man superior to him, like the winner in a child's game of hide-and-seek! This common idea is the root of all idol worship and false religion, for man then sees himself as his own saviour, and as the ultimate object of his worship. Paganism is the fruit of a false idea of love, while true religion is the fruit of a genuine, heavenly idea of love.

4. *Natural human love depends on the value of its object.* We all treat wealthy, powerful people with more respect than we normally show to the rubbish collector. The prophet David (Daud) writes of Allah, "Even though you are so high above, You care for the lowly."[8] This kind of love is foreign to this evil world. Allah's love actually *creates* value in its object. A human being is transformed when he receives and believes the love of Allah for him. This is true religion.

Pick up an ordinary stone lying on the ground. It is so worthless that you could not sell it anywhere, even for a copper coin. But if you could love that stone the way a mother loves her baby, and in so doing transform it into a piece of solid gold, you could then sell it for a fortune. This is what Allah's heavenly love does for us poor, unworthy mortals: "I will make a man more precious than fine gold; even a man than the golden wedge of Ophir."[9] Praise be to him for his *creative*

---

7. Luke 19:10.
8. Psalm 138:6, TEV.
9. Isaiah 13:12.

love! This is the reason why Allah must be our Saviour. Man cannot save himself because he has no natural-born love like that of Allah. For this reason he cannot transform his impure, selfish nature.

5. *Ordinary human love is possessive by nature.* Even sexual love is highly acquisitive. We speak of a friendship with a person as something we have acquired, something added to our possessions. It enriches us. By contrast, Allah's great love is not acquisitive in nature. The reason he loves us is not because he wants to get something out of us, so as to enrich himself. This amazing reversal of the ancient values of human love is seen in the words of Jesus (Issa).

> When you give a feast, invite the poor, the crippled, the lame, and the blind; ... they are not able to pay you back.[10]

The Holy Injil portrays the character of Allah in a much more glorious light than the ancient Jews were able to perceive it. A kind, compassionate, loving father does not seek to enrich himself at the expense of his children; rather, he will give himself for them, even dying if necessary in order to save their lives. so Allah is revealed as One who gives himself for those who worship him, and not as one who selfishly enriches himself at their expense. Such love is the credential of divine character. Love like this is a miracle, for it has no human origins.

6. *When examined closely, ordinary human love proves to be nothing other than self-love.* Many godless people have praised self-love as being a fine thing. The ancient Greeks considered it to be the highest form of human goodness; but those ancient Greeks were pagans, and we must reject the new paganism of self-worship which is sweeping our modern world. It cannot redeem society because the root of society's problem is selfishness. How can more of the same sickness possibly cure a disease?

---

10. Luke 14:13, TEV.

A clear example of the contrast between human love and God's love is seen in comparing ancient Greek love with what is proclaimed by the Injil. The pagan Greeks had a favourite story. A certain hero, Admetus, became very ill. The pagan "gods" decreed that he must die unless someone could be found willing to die in his place. His friends asked various ones if they would be willing to die for Admetus. No one volunteered. Then they came to his own parents. "Would you die for your son, that he might live?"

"Oh," they replied, "we love our son very much; but sorry, we could not die for him."

Finally they came to his wife, Alcestis. Her response was like this: "Admetus is such a good man, so noble, so valuable to the world, that, yes, I will die in his place!" The Greeks hailed this as the supreme manifestation of love, the greatest the world could see—someone willing to die for a good man. They could imagine nothing better!

Allah's love is different and more wonderful. The apostles of Jesus "turned the world upside down" with this astounding, revolutionary idea of love:

> It is a difficult thing for someone to die for a righteous person. It may even be that someone might dare to die for a good [valuable, beautiful] person. But God has shown us how much he loves us—it was while we were still sinners. ... We were God's enemies, but he made us his friends.[11]

Over thousands of years, many stories and dramas had been written by the ancients, including the Jews; but no one had ever conceived of love such as this! This was the most amazing idea ever proclaimed in the world, and it is still a wonder to earth's millions. This is why the enemies of the apostles complained, "These that have turned the world upside down are come hither also."[12] The, power was not in

---

5. Romans 5:7-10, TEV.
6. Acts 17:6, TEV.

the sword, nor in higher education, but in love. That new idea of love was embodied in the apostles' little word *agape*, a word that was like dynamite. *Agape* is a Greek word that is not very well known in the world today, and it describes a type of love that is also not very well known. That *agape* love did a great work in the days of the apostles. It divided humanity into two camps, one transformed into joyous followers of Jesus, and the other into their implacable enemies. None who heard the news about *agape* could be neutral!

But wait, the most amazing contrast is yet to come!

7. *Ordinary human love always wants to rise up higher, to climb to greater heights.* Sometimes this is called "progress", but often it means climbing over other people in our push to improve our own situation. Seldom do we see a politician who is at the head of a state or in a high office, who is willing to voluntarily step down to a lower position. Seldom do we see a rich man willing to return to the levels of poverty where his career began. Human nature wants to climb higher.

God's love is not a sentimental, weak emotion. It is as tough as steel and utterly demanding. Nevertheless, it is the direct opposite of man's natural "climb up higher" desire; it dares to step down lower, and still lower, in order to ransom wandering human beings.

We shall see this kind of love revealed, but let us first find out who it was that invented man's natural idea of self-seeking and climbing up higher.

It was Iblis himself. Satan was once an angel in heaven, but something went wrong with him. Allah said of him:

> Thou sealest up the sum, full of wisdom, and perfect in beauty. Thou hast been in Eden the garden of God. ... The workmanship of thy tabrets and of thy pipes was prepared in thee in the day that thou wast created. Thou art the anointed cherub that covereth; and I have set thee so: thou wast upon the holy mountain of God; thou hast walked up and down

in the midst of the stones of fire. Thou wast perfect in thy ways from the day that thou wast created, till iniquity was found in thee.[13]

Clearly, words like these could be said of no other one than Satan (Iblis) himself! What was the "iniquity" that was "found" in him? How did he change from a pure, perfect angel to the horrible adversary of Allah and man that he is now?

The prophet Isaiah tells us the story. Note the five instances that Lucifer, who became Satan, proudly talked about himself ("I") as his supreme object of worship; and the five times he talked about climbing up higher (the expressions will be emphasized so you can catch them readily):

> How art thou fallen from heaven, O Lucifer, son of the morning! how art thou cut down to the ground, which didst weaken the nations! For thou hast said in thine heart, *I* will *ascend* into heaven, *I* will *exalt* my throne above the stars of God: *I* will sit also upon the *mount* of the congregation, in the sides of the North: *I* will *ascend* above the heights of the clouds; *I* will be like the *most High*. Yet thou shalt be brought down to hell, to the sides of the pit.[14]

When Adam yielded to evil temptation in the beginning, it caused a change in human nature, with man becoming like Iblis in aim and character. Every human being who is intent on his own pride, seeking to push himself higher and still higher, is simply following his lead. This can be seen everywhere, and is Satan's invention: The love of self. No baby ever cries because some other baby is hungry for milk—he cries for himself. Man is born self-centred.

If there were no true religion to counteract this natural-born love of self, we would reveal this natural selfishness in many ugly ways as we grew older. Greed, lust, materialism, hatred, wars, sensuality; the list of manifestations is endless.

---

13. Ezekiel 28:12-15.
14. Isaiah 14:12-15, emphases supplied.

As each human being looks at himself, he is compelled to recognize this as a picture of his own heart, were it not for the mercy of Allah.

The love of Allah for the world must reverse this selfish spirit of Iblis! It must reverse this universal human process that is so productive of injustice, suffering, and pain. It must undo the sin of selfishness. Forgiveness is much more than a mere pardoning of evil while continuing to tolerate it. True forgiveness undoes the evil, and changes the heart. Allah's love is not the selfish kind of "climb-up-higher" love that Iblis revealed; instead, it is a love that dares to step down lower, a love that knows no cowardly, selfish fear. It is powerful.

Except by revealing this kind of love, there was no other way that Allah could untie the knot of sin that Iblis had tied. Even angels were amazed to behold Allah's demonstration of a kind of love undreamed of through all the past ages of eternity.

Did Hazrat Abraham begin to see the unfolding of this great divine love in his day, long ago? Yes, he did; and we must continue to search for its meaning.

"O true believers, eat of the good things which we have bestowed on you for food, and return thanks unto God, if ye serve Him. Verily, He hath forbidden you to eat that which dieth of itself, and blood and swine's flesh, and that on which any other name but Allah's hath been invoked."

(*The Qur'an*, 2:172, 173).

7
Allah's Way to Health, Happiness, and Longer Life

Allah's mercy and compassion lead him to care for even the little creatures that he has created. The prophet David (Daud) says that he opens his hand to "satisfy the desires of every living thing."[1] Since we humans are infinitely more valuable than birds or animals, we can assume that he also wants us to be healthy, happy, and to enjoy long life. He was concerned for the health and happiness of his "friend" Abraham.

The Holy Book likewise expresses Allah's concern for our health and happiness: "Dear friend, I pray that you may enjoy good health, and that all may go well with you, even as your soul is getting along well."[2]

Everyone desires that "all may go well with" him, and no one wants things to go wrong. If you bought a new car, you would be very sorry to see it wrecked and declared an insurance write-off long before you had got your use out of it. How much more tragic when our bodies get "wrecked"

---

1. Psalm 145:16, NIV.
2. 3 John 2, NIV.

through sickness, and our life is cut short long before it should be. Someone about to die will usually be prepared to give all his or her wealth in order to be well again.

Some say it is "the will of Allah" when they get sick and die prematurely like the people of Somalia, South Sudan, Yemen and Syria, where thousands have suffered from drought- and war-inflicted famine. They shrug their shoulders and say, "We are doomed unless Allah wills to rescue us." Droughts and famines have never been Allah's will for any people; man himself has ruined his environment and invited disasters.

Would it not be foolishness, yes, even blasphemy, for a drunkard who wrecks his new car, and thereby squanders his family's possessions, to claim that it is the will of Allah that this calamity should have happened? Did he ask Allah whether he should drink alcohol? Did he listen to Allah's word? If we learn to take care of our bodies as he has commanded us in his Word, it is much less likely that we will get sick or die prematurely.

In the light of these facts, is it right to say that it is Allah's will for any of us to destroy our health and make ourselves sick? If you drive your new car wisely and take proper care of it, it will be likely to give you long service. Your body is worth infinitely more. If we follow the divine directions, we too may live long lives and realize the truth of Allah's promise: "The hoary head [white with age] is a crown of glory, if it be found in the way of righteousness."[3]

There are young people who carelessly gamble away their health and even their lives. They say, "I don't mind if I die young. Nobody cares about me anyway. I'll just burn my life-candle at both ends, and if I die soon—so what! I belong to myself anyway." They are mistaken. They do not belong to themselves. We read in the honoured Qur'an that when Allah

---

3. Proverbs 16:31.

commanded Abraham to offer his son, he himself provided "a tremendous Victim" in order to redeem the boy.[4] The redemption price was blood. That same price has been paid for today's youth. They are the property of a kind and loving Allah who wants them to be happy and healthy. Many more of today's youth would be happy if only they understood that they don't belong to themselves. They are loved!

The light that glows from Abraham's great sacrifice shines down the ages for us today. One of Jesus' (Issa's) apostles says, "Because of God's great mercy to us I appeal to you: offer yourselves as a living sacrifice to God, dedicated to his service and pleasing to him. This is the true worship that you should offer."[5] Allah did not desire a dead son from Abraham; neither does he desire your death, or that you should be a sick or unhappy person. "A living sacrifice" is a happy one: a healthy, prosperous, long life offered as true worship to the One who has blessed us so abundantly. The care of our health is therefore both a duty and a pleasure!

All who worship God in truth know and believe themselves to be Abraham's descendants, for he is "the father of all that believe." They will therefore have a vital sense of self-respect. It is impossible for anyone who believes Allah's love to regard himself or herself carelessly by descending to the use of degrading liquors or drugs.

If some infidel were to dump a load of rubbish in the sacred mosque, those who worship God would be highly indignant, and rightly so. There is something just as bad that is happening every day, all around the world: people are defiling their bodies, the wonderful creation of Allah!

The great prophet Daniel was faced with the temptation to eat food or to imbibe drink that would be harmful to the body that Allah had given him. We read that he "purposed in

---

4. *The Qur'an*, 37:107.
5. Romans 12:1, TEV.

his heart that he would not "defile himself" with the "portion of the king's meat [food]," and "with the wine which he drank."[6] He was a true son of Abraham; he realized that if he ate that kind of food which is harmful to health, he would be dumping rubbish into the body which Allah had created for him.

How can one defile his body?

The use of harmful, unclean food or drink defiles it. "Whether therefore ye eat, or drink, or whatsoever ye do, do all to the glory of God."[7] Allah's will for our healthful, happy living is expressed as follows:

The use of all intoxicating liquors is forbidden. Here are just a few of the divine warnings against this evil:

> Wine is a mocker, and beer a brawler; whoever is led astray by them is not wise.[8]

> Be not among winebibbers; among riotous eaters of flesh: for the drunkard and the glutton shall come to poverty.[9]

Every descendant of Abraham is a "king" in Allah's eyes, someone important. Note how he guides us:

> It is not for kings, O Lemuel—not for kings to drink wine, not for rulers to crave beer, lest they drink and forget what the law decrees, and deprive all the oppressed of their rights Give beer to those who are perishing, wine to those who are in anguish, let them drink and forget their poverty and remember their misery no more.[10]

Let us not misunderstand this very wise counsel. The Book is not giving encouragement to poor people to drink and forget their misery! By no means. It is pointing out, through

---

6. Daniel 1:8.
7. 1 Corinthians 10:31.
8. Proverbs 20:1, NIV.
9. Proverbs 23:20, 21.
10. Proverbs 31:4-7, NIV.

a figure of speech known as irony, the folly of many who do just that, thereby driving themselves further into misery and poverty, like a car that spins its wheels ever deeper into mud. Such persons are not Abraham's descendants by faith. Beer and wine are no solution to life's problems. There is no difficulty so bad but that alcohol can make it worse:

> Who has woe? Who has sorrow? Who has strife? Who has complaints? Who has needless bruises? Who has bloodshot eyes? Those who linger over wine, who go to sample bowls of mixed wine. ... In the end it bites like a snake and poisons like a viper. Your eyes will see strange sights and your mind imagine confusing things. You will be like one sleeping on the high seas, lying on top of the rigging [a most dangerous place to be!]. "They hit me," you will say, "but I am not hurt! They beat me, but I don't feel it! When will I wake up so I can find another drink?"[11]

It is pitiful and tragic that a human being can so degrade himself that he actually welcomes such self-punishment and then asks for more! The condition described here fits drug addiction as readily as it fits alcoholism. "Woe to those who rise early in the morning to run after their drinks, who stay up late at night till they are inflamed with wine. ... They have no regard for the deeds of the Lord, no respect for the work of his hands."[12] *This* is defiling the body—having "no respect for the work of his hands."

Allah forbids any of his people to serve alcoholic drinks to anyone else: "Woe to him who gives drink to his neighbours, pouring it from the wineskin till they are drunk ."[13] This is because of his great principle of love.[14]

---

11. Proverbs 23:29-35, NIV.
12. Isaiah 5:11, 12, NIV.
13. Habakkuk 2:15, NIV.
14. Matthew 7:11, NIV.

What a terrible account bartenders, barmaids, and hosts and hostesses who serve liquor, will face in the Judgment Day! The liquor they have served has injured the people who drank it, and in many cases even led to crime and murder. Even wise men and judges have wronged innocent people because of drinking. "Priests and prophets stagger from beer and are befuddled with wine; they reel from beer, they stagger when seeing visions, they stumble when rendering decisions."[15] Kingdoms and empires have been defeated because their rulers were drunk when attacked by invading armies. The fall of Babylon is one such example: Belshazzar, the last king, was drunk the night that the Medo-Persian soldiers stealthily entered the capital. The king was drunk when a rebel soldier plunged a sword through his heart, thus ending the world's wealthiest empire.[16]

Allah's Word says that "drunkards" will not inherit Paradise. The honoured Qur'an speaks of the sin of drinking: "They ask thee about intoxicants (al-khamr) and games of chance, Say: In both of them is a great sin."[17] Maulana Muhammad Ali explains this:

> "'Khamr' means wine or grapewine, ... anything or any intoxicating thing that clouds or obscures (literally, covers) the intellect. ... The Khamr includes all intoxicating substances. ... The prohibition spoken of here as regards both intoxicating liquors and games of chance is made plainer in 5:90: 'O you who believe, intoxicants and games of chance ... are only an uncleanness, the devil's work; shun it therefore that you may be successful.'"[18]

One of the greatest social miracles that ever took place on earth was the tremendous change in the Arab tribes due

---

16. See *World Book Encyclopedia*, vol. 2, p. 193 (1978 ed.).
17. *The Qur'an*, "The Cow," 2:219, 220.
18. *The Qur'an*, 5:90.

to Prophet Muhammad's teachings about wine. Maulana Muhammad Ali tells what happened:

> The change which these simple words [of the Qur'an] brought about in Arabia will always remain a riddle to the social reformer. The constant fighting of Arab tribes one against the other had made the habit of drink second nature to the Arab, and wine was one of the very few objects which could furnish a topic to the mind of an Arab poet. Intoxicating liquors were the chief feature of their feasts, and the habit of drink was not looked upon as an evil, nor had there ever been a temperance movement among them, the Jews and the Christians being themselves addicted to this evil. Human experience with regard to the habit of drink is that of all evils it is the most difficult to be uprooted.
>
> Yet, but one word of the Holy Qur'an was sufficient to blot out all traces of it from among a whole nation, and afterwards from the whole of the country as it came over to Islam. History cannot present another instance of a wonderful transformation of this magnitude brought about so easily yet so thoroughly.
>
> It may also be added here that Sale's remark that "the moderate use of wine is allowed" and that only drinking to excess is prohibited, according to some, is absolutely without foundation. The companions of the Prophet never made use of a drop of wine after the prohibition was made known.[19]

It is related that when the words of the honoured Qur'an were proclaimed by a crier in the streets of Medina, there was an immediate response of the people. Every jar of wine in the Muslim houses was emptied, so that wine flowed in the streets.[20]

It is a mistake to assume that the Holy Injil permitted the use of alcoholic drinks. Christians who drink, even moderately

---

19. Idem.
20. Al Jami' al Musnad al Sahih (Hadith) by Al-Iman Abu 'abd Allah Muhammad Ibn Ismail al-Bukhari, 43:22.

as they suppose, are going contrary to the teachings of the Bible they profess to obey; and they have departed from the pure teachings of Jesus. He said: "Be careful, or your hearts will be weighed down with dissipation, drunkenness and the anxieties of life, and that day [of Judgment] will close on you unexpectedly like a trap. For it will come upon all those who live on the face of the whole earth. Be always on the watch."[21]

But, say some, did not Jesus actually perform a miracle to make fermented wine? And did he not serve such to his own disciples? No! Some have mistakenly understood these incidents to give them license to drink.

The word "wine" had two meanings: either referring to fermented wine, which was alcoholic and intoxicating; or unfermented wine, which was the healthful, non-alcoholic kind of fruit juice. The ancient Romans called the latter *mustum*, made from pressing fresh juice from grapes. Different kinds of grape juice could be blended with spices added for flavour. The ancient "pause that refreshes" was this kind of non-alcoholic drink.

Those people knew very well how to bottle mustum so that it would be kept pure for as long as a year without fermenting. They used tall earthenware jars known as amphora which were corked tightly so as to remain air-tight. The wine did not ferment and was called *aei gleukos* in Greek, or *sempe mustum* in Latin. Alcoholic wine was called *oionos tropias* in Greek, but the expression is not found in the New Testament.

The famous "Last Supper" was instituted during the Jewish Passover time when leaven and intoxicants were forbidden, and therefore the "wine" used had to be non-alcoholic. It was called "This fruit of the vine," an expression that could mean only an unfermented drink.[22] And Jesus

---

21. Luke 21:34-36, NIV.
22. Matthew 26:29.

would never have changed the water at Cana's wedding feast into an intoxicating drink when the Holy Book condemned intoxication of any kind.

There is another harmful substance that many people are using today: tobacco. It is an evil that was not invented in ancient times. If anything, it is even more harmful than the use of alcohol.

Suppose an airline should try to solicit your patronage with advertising that boldly declares that one out of three passengers who travel on their planes will die in air accidents. Would you buy a ticket from them? No! Yet it is a clear fact that one out of three people who smoke regularly will eventually die from the effects of their cigarettes; while the health and quality of life of the other two are adversely affected as well.

Scientists have called cigarette addiction "slow-motion suicide." The British Royal College of Physicians has said that each cigarette cuts five and a half minutes from the smoker's life. That is one reason why you hear of so many people dying of various diseases in their 40's and 50's, long before their proper time has come. Death often strikes them just as they stand on the verge of attaining their ambitions—those accumulative five and half minutes are suddenly subtracted in one lump sum: death by cancer or coronary failure. Thirty or forty extra years of happy life are gone, and now they must lie in the ground instead.

Health authorities in one Western nation, the USA, estimate that between 360,000 and 400,000 people there die every year from the effects of cigarette smoking.[23] As a result, the Western tobacco companies are now beginning to meet stiff opposition to their death-dealing commodity, and are turning to Africa and the Third World to recoup their sagging profits. Reports John Madeley from London:

---

23. *Reader's Digest,* "Nicotine: Profile of Peril," by S.S. Field, September 1973, pp. 77-80, USA edition.

People in developing countries are, it seems, being persuaded by advertising which implies that affluent people normally smoke—which is not true in the West. WHO (World Health Organization) reports that non-smokers outnumber smokers in Britain, the United States, Sweden, Norway, and other Western countries.... The tobacco industry in Nigeria is said by WHO to have launched a "massive marketing campaign."[24]

The same author reports on tests that indicate that cigarettes sold in Britain and the United States contain less than a quarter of the nicotine content of those sold in the Third World, and about half the amount of tar. In other words, the Third World is being exploited!

All who have a regard for the Word of Allah will never use tobacco or any such poison or harmful drug, for the very good reason that they regard the care of their bodies as a sacred responsibility.

Dr. Alexander Jakubovic, a Canadian biochemist, has studied the effects of THC (the ingredient in bhang or marijuana (pot) that produces the so-called "high"). He is convinced that this drug is harmful to the brains of both teenagers and adults. Dr. Robert Heath, a neurologist, has conducted experiments on monkeys' brains and found that THC hastens aging in the nerve cell nuclei.

Dr. Harris Rosenkrants studied the effects of marijuana on rats and found that their lungs were damaged more by it than by tobacco smoke. Dr. Donald Taskin, a specialist in lung diseases, studied 74 men who smoke bhang and found that "heavy pot smoking does something to the larger airways [of the lungs] that tobacco smoking doesn't do." Bhang is a "flight from reality" and from Allah. It is a deceptive attempt to find peace. It's like taking an aspirin in order to forget the pain of cancer, instead of having surgery to remove the cancer. It

---

24. *The London Observer Service.*

becomes a path to death. God loves you as an individual. Why ruin your life by drugs?

Swine's flesh and other unclean meats are prohibited by the God of Abraham. Yet the world is thousands of years behind in accepting this counsel from Allah.

Moses was "learned in all the wisdom of the Egyptians."[25] Doubtless he knew of the foolish medical remedies prescribed by the best physicians of Egypt, as recorded in the "Papyrus Ebers" (an Egyptian medical work of about 1,500 B.C.). For example, this so-called "wisdom" prescribes magic water which had been poured over a heathen idol as the cure for the victims of a poisonous snake bite. It even prescribed the use of animals' excreta!

But Moses turned from all this foolishness and let God teach him true wisdom. He tells us that eating swine's flesh is unhealthful, along with fish that do not have fins and scales. Generally speaking, the creatures that Allah pronounced unclean are scavengers either on earth, in the sky, or in the seas. The details of this legislation are in the Torah.[26]

Before the Flood, the prophet Noah (Nuhu) knew the distinction between clean and unclean animals, because God sent the clean animals into the ark by sevens and the unclean ones by twos. After the Flood, only the clean animals were used for sacrifices. Naturally, Abraham's sacrifices were always according to divine law, for we know that Allah trusted him to "keep the way of the Lord, to do justice and judgment."[27] Can he trust you in the same way?

The ancients may not have known of a scientific reason why Allah prohibited the use of these unclean foods, but modern medical science has enlightened us. There is a disease in pork induced by *trichinella spiralis*, tiny microscopic worms that

---

25. Acts 7:22.
26. Leviticus 11:2-9.
27. Genesis 18:19.

come from improperly cooked pork which burrow their way into the muscles of humans. The larvae can invade important parts of the body and cause serious diseases. Doctors are often fooled by this disease and diagnose their patients wrongly.

Dr. Maurice Hall, formerly of the Public Health Department in the USA, once said that most cases of trichinosis are missed by the physician. There is wisdom in the words found in the Qur'an:

> Forbidden unto you for food are carrion and blood and swine's flesh and that which had been dedicated unto any other than God.[28]

Some followers of the Christ have the mistaken notion that their leader cleansed the hogs so that they can now be eaten.[29] We know this cannot be true. A Biblical description of the Judgment Day tells how "those who ... eat the flesh of pigs and rats ... will meet their end together." There are many of the people of the Book who follow the truth taught therein, and who never eat pork or other unclean foods.[30]

The reason why a true worshipper of Allah will not use these forbidden things is because he wants to keep his mind

---

28. The Qur'an, 5:3.

29. Many who profess to follow the teachings of the Holy Bible transgress its true teachings, not only in using alcoholic drinks and swine's flesh and other unclean meats, but in eating blood. They are unaware that Jesus' apostles, in conformity with the teachings of the Holy Bible, expressly forbade eating flesh in which is blood: "You are to abstain from food sacrificed to idols, from blood, from meat of strangled animals, and from sexual immorality." (Acts 15:28, 29, NIV).

30. They are known as Seventh-day Adventists. Many who believe the New Testament teachings have become vegetarians partly because of this word concerning unclean foods, and partly in the desire to return (for the sake of better health) as nearly as possible to the diet that Allah gave man in the beginning at creation (see Genesis 1:29; 3:18). Seventh-day Adventists teach the benefits of a vegetarian diet, and they certainly teach the evil of eating blood, which Allah has forbidden.

and body in the best possible condition. Think of a radio that is finely tuned and in perfect working order: it is sensitive enough to catch important broadcasts. If it is not in good condition, it cannot "hear" the voices sent through the air by other electronic equipment.

In a more real sense than with radio or TV transmissions, the compassionate Allah is sending a message of redemption to the whole world in these important times. Unfortunately, many people cannot "hear" because their minds are confused by the use of improper food and drink, and poisonous substances.

Our eternal security depends on our having the true faith of Abraham.

"Is our power exhausted by the first creation? Yea, they are in perplexity, because of a new creation which is foretold them, namely the raising of the dead. We created man, and We know what his soul whispereth within him; and We are nearer unto him than his jugular vein."

(*The Qur'an*, 50:15, 16).

8

Can We Know What Lies Beyond Death?

We know incomparably more about the mysteries of the human body, even the electrical energy of the human nervous system, than did our ancient ancestors. At the opposite side of the spectrum of human knowledge, we know much more about the planets, stars and galaxies in the far-flung universe than they knew. In between the mysteries of our own human bodies and the mysteries of space there is a tremendous field of scientific knowledge now open to our understanding.

There is one area, however, that all of man's scientific discovery has not been able to penetrate: the mystery of death. Some people who have started to die have been rescued by medical science before their inner mental processes became completely defunct. They have told us of their feelings and "visions" while in this dying state, but no one who has actually died has ever returned to tell us what lies beyond.

Death is more remote than Saturn or Mars: a "barrier", says the honoured Qur'an, beyond which we cannot conduct any valid experiments.[1] Speculation or philosophy is at its best, only guess-work. Our human imaginings about what lies beyond death can in fact be harmful, because they can be inspired by the enemy, Iblis. Our only source of accurate knowledge about death is what Allah has revealed to us.

If we believe the truth, it will provide us with comfort, peace, and confidence for the future. If we disbelieve it, then like a foolish ship's captain we have cut our moorings and will drift aimlessly in an ocean of suppositions with fear as our only pilot.

Let us note the clear truths about what lies beyond death, as we find them in Allah's revealed truth:

1. *Allah loves each of his faithful ones personally and individually, so that it is he who wants them to be with him in eternity.* It is *he* who wants his children to be resurrected from the dead, like parents who cannot bear to be separated from their child forever. Therefore, the resurrection from the dead will take place because "God is love." *We* are the lost children who will be brought back again from the land of death, and the resurrection will be at *his* initiative.

The first man who seems to have understood this great truth was the patriarch Job (Ayyub). He did not know that it was Satan (Iblis) who had sent him all his terrible troubles; he thought it was Allah. He knew Allah to be kind and merciful, and he could not reason out why Allah had turned against him so bitterly. In Job chapter 14 the pathetic sufferer sees himself as a little boy who welcomes his usually loving father home from his day's work, throwing himself into his father's arms with delight. But instead of father being kind as he usually is, something strange has happened—father is drunk and angry. He flings his little "boy" Job cruelly aside, cursing and abusing him. Poor Job runs away to hide in a dark room until his father's strange fit is over. Notice carefully what Job

---

1. *The Qur'an*, 23:99, 100

says. He has no Book such as a copy of the Qur'an or a Bible to read; he doesn't know or understand what we do today; but he begins to see the resurrection from the dead as an expression of Allah's love:

> I wish you would hide me in the world of the dead; let me be hidden until your anger is over, and then set a time to remember me. If a man dies, can he come back to life? But I will wait for better times, wait till this time of trouble is ended. Then you will call, and I will answer, and you will be pleased with me.[2]

A little later Job says that Allah is his Friend and Saviour, who will resurrect him from the dead:

> I know that my Redeemer lives, and that in the end he will stand upon the earth. And after my skin has been destroyed, yet in my flesh I will see God, I myself will see him with my own eyes—I, and not another. How my heart yearns within me![3]

2. *Death is a quiet, peaceful rest in sleep, awaiting the resurrection.* When his friend Lazarus had died, Jesus (Issa) said of him, "'Our friend Lazarus has fallen asleep; but I am going there to wake him up.'" His disciples understood him to mean that Lazarus had not died, but that he had found relief from his fever by normal sleep. The Holy Injil continues:

> Jesus had been speaking of his death, but his disciples thought he meant natural sleep.
>
> So then he told them plainly, "Lazarus is dead, and for your sake I am glad I was not there, so that you may believe. But let us go to him."[4]

The great prophet Daniel teaches the same truth: "Multitudes who sleep in the dust of the earth will awake: some to everlasting life, others to shame and everlasting contempt."[5]

---

2. Job 14:13-15, TEV.
3. Job 19:25-27 NIV.
4. John 11:11-15 NIV.
5. Daniel 12:2, NIV.

The Holy Injil is consistent and clear:

> Brothers, we do not want you to be ignorant about those who fall asleep, or to grieve like the rest of men, who have no hope. ...We who are still alive, who are left till the coming of the Lord, will certainly not precede those who have fallen asleep. For the Lord himself will come down from heaven, with a loud command, with the voice of the archangel and with the trumpet call. of God, and the dead in Christ will rise first.[6]

The honoured Qur'an is clear that there is a "barrier" that prevents any contact between the living and the dead. The reason is that the dead are asleep and are therefore not conscious:

> When death comes to one of them, he says, "My Lord, send me back, that I may do right in that which I have left behind." But, no, it is but a word he speaks; and there behind them is a barrier until the day that they shall be raised up.[7]

When we go to sleep at night, we know nothing until we awaken the next morning and hear the birds singing again. So also with the believer who lies down in death. He may have died thousands of years ago, but his rest is to him but a moment, like the wink of an eye. Yet all the while he has been under the watch-care of his loving Allah, like a child asleep on its mother's breast. The Qur'an says:

> He will say, "How long have you tarried in the grave, counting by years?" They will say, "We have tarried but a day, or part of a day, ask of those who keep count." He will say, "You have tarried but a little if you only knew."[8]

The condition in death is no more painful than a restful sleep that intervenes before the resurrection:

---

6. 1 Thessalonians 4:13-16, NIV.
7. *The Qur'an*, 23:99, 100.
8. *The Qur'an*, 23:112-114.

Don't put your trust in human leaders; no human being can save you. When they die, they return to the dust; on that day all their plans come to an end.[9]

A live dog is better off than a dead lion. Yes, the living know they are going to die, but the dead know nothing. They have no further reward; they are completely forgotten. Their loves, their hates, their passions, all died with them. They will never again take part in anything that happens in this world [until the resurrection, that is]. ... There will be no action, no thought, no knowledge, no wisdom in the world of the dead.[10]

3. *This means, of course, that all attempts to communicate with the dead are in fact heathenism.* No mortal has the ability to break through that "barrier" of death, or to awaken the dead out of their sleep. Allah has not given that power to anyone. Any witch, necromancer, or spiritist medium who claims a power that God has not given, is either telling us a lie or is under the control of Satan.

Some may say: "But the spirit mediums do communicate with the dead! They bring them back, and we see them, and actually hear their voices. We recognize them!" Allah has clearly and repeatedly forbidden his faithful people to have anything to do with spirit mediums or witches.[11] King Saul of Israel was condemned to the last Judgment because his final act of rebellion against God was to consult a medium who deceived him into thinking she had brought Samuel "up" from the dead.[12] Satan and his clever angels were once mighty and intelligent beings in heaven. They have the skill to counterfeit the appearance and even the voices of our dead

---

9. Psalm 146:3, 4, TEV.

10. Ecclesiastes 9:4, 5, 10, TEV.

11. See Isaiah 8:19; Leviticus 19:31; 20:26; Exodus 22:18; Deuteronomy 18:10-12; 32:17.

12. 1 Samuel 28:8, 7-14; 1 Chronicles 10:13, 14.

loved ones. We all know of actors who can do this fairly well; surely Satan is much more clever than they are!

> They are spirits of demons performing miraculous signs, and they go out to the kings of the whole world.[13]

> Satan himself masquerades as an angel of light. It is not surprising, then, if his servants masquerade as servants of righteousness.[14]

Like Abraham, none who choose to believe the Word of Allah will be deceived by these Satanic impostors; but it is sad to see that many are being deceived today because they do not want to know the truth. They sell their souls for a little human gain, snatching the bait of the tempter and getting caught like a fish on a hook. Thank God for the truth revealed in his holy Word! Accept it wholeheartedly and it will forever deliver you from fear.

Two ideas about the dead have contended against each other ever since sin began. The Bible says that Allah told Adam and his wife that they should not eat of the fruit of the forbidden tree, "for in the day that thou eatest thereof thou shalt surely die." Satan said: "Ye shall not surely die."[15] Shall we believe Satan's lie?

The other idea is the truth as revealed by Allah himself: man's nature is mortal; our life is borrowed, derived, a gift from Allah. Our only hope, therefore, of eternal life, is in him.

The Word explains this very clearly:

> And the Lord God formed man of the dust of the ground, and breathed into his nostrils the breath of life; and man became a living soul.[16]

---

13. Revelation 16:14, NIV.
14. 2 Corinthians 11:14, 15, NIV.
15. Genesis. 2:17; 3:4.
16. Genesis 2:7.

Thus the soul is composed of the union of the body plus the breath, or spark of life that comes only from God. A wooden box is composed of assembled boards and nails. A pile of boards on one side and nails on the other would not be a box. As soon as you pull out the nails, and separate the boards the box ceases to exist.

So with man: he was formed "a living soul." When he dies, the "breath" leaves and the body goes back to dust again, to await the resurrection day when God shall re-create it.

The teaching of the natural immortality of the soul has been associated with idolatry and heathenism since earliest times.

4. *The resurrection will take place at the last day.* Jesus (Issa) promised to return, and said that the reason for his coming was to renew fellowship with those who are true believers:

> Believe in God and believe also in me. ... I am going to prepare a place for you. I would not tell you this if it were not so. And after I go and prepare a place for you, I will come back and take you to myself, so that you will be where I am.[17]

Those whom he promises to "take" to himself are both the living and the resurrected saints.

Neither the righteous nor the wicked go to their reward immediately at death. All go to sleep; and the reward will come at the resurrection when both believers and unbelievers will rise again. Let us read in the honoured Qur'an:

> How do you disbelieve in God seeing you were dead and He gave you life, then He shall make you dead, then He shall give you life, then unto Him you shall be returned.[18]

> And afterward, when He calls you, once and suddenly, out of the earth you will emerge.[19]

---

17. John 14:1-3, TEV.
18. *The Qur'an*, 2:28.
19. *The Qur'an* 30:25.

When we say good-bye to a loved one who is dying, we have a joyous hope and confidence in the promises of God. Listen to what the Holy Injil says:

> Listen, I tell you a mystery: We will not all sleep, but we will all be changed—in a flash, in the twinkling of an eye, at the last trumpet. For the trumpet will sound, the dead will be raised imperishable, and we will be changed. For the perishable must clothe itself with the imperishable, and the mortal with immortality.[20]

And again we consult the honoured Qur'an:

And the trumpet shall be blown; then behold, from the graves they come unto their Lord crying, Woe unto us, who has roused us from our place of sleep?[21]

It will, however, not be "woe" for those who are roused from their sleep by the voice of God if they have gone to sleep in true faith: "All that are in the graves shall hear his voice."[22] It will be a voice full of music and happiness that awakes them. They will enjoy eternal fellowship with Allah and with his people from all ages, for he will create for them "a new heaven and a new earth, the home of righteousness."[23] This is Paradise.

5. *Every human soul will meet God face to face in a final Judgment.* Not one who died faithless is now suffering the torture of fire. Scripture teaches a truth that is clear and reasonable, that appeals to our sense of fairness on the part of Allah. All are resting in the "sleep" that we call death until the resurrection; *then* will come the Judgment. Even then, those who have chosen not to believe the good news of truth that God sends will not be unendingly tortured for eternal ages by a cruel and bloodthirsty God. Scripture teaches that "the wages of

---

20. 1 Corinthians 15:51-53, NIV.
21. The Qur'an, 36:51, 52.
22. John 5:28.
23. 2 Peter 3:13, NIV. See Revelation chapters 21 and 22.

sin is death," [24] not an eternal life of torture. Note the sensible words of Christ:

> As the weeds are pulled up and burned in the fire, so it will be at the end of the age. ... Angels ... will weed out of his kingdom everything that causes sin and all who do evil. They will throw them into the fiery furnace, where there will be weeping and gnashing of teeth.[25]

That "fiery furnace" will not burn on for ever and ever. It will consume them as "stubble" in the fire, and "shall leave them neither root not branch."[26] Allah, the kind and compassionate One, must punish sin, rebellion and unbelief; but he still delights in mercy. He is not a cruel sadist who enjoys seeing the creatures he created suffer endless agony.

Those who have rebelled against him and rejected his forgiveness would not find any happiness in the heavenly Paradise he has prepared for his children. It would be torture for them to prolong their lives forever. We see therefore, that in mercy and kindness to them, he permits their unhappy lives to be cut off.

If by accident one incorrigible rebel found himself in Paradise, he would be unhappy there and would surely head for the nearest exit! The lost are not shut out of heaven by any harsh decree from Allah himself, but by their own unworthiness for the pure and holy companionship to be found there. Allah does not want any of us to dread death or the Day of Judgment as something that will be "against" us. The Holy Injil presents the "good news" of a God who is compassionate, loving, and always seeking the eternal good of all mankind:

---

24. Romans 6:23.
25. Matthew 13:40-42, NIV.
26. Malachi 4:1.

> The light shines in the darkness, but the darkness has not overcome [margin] it. ... The true light ... gives light to every man.[27]

> This is the verdict: Light has come into the world, but men loved darkness instead of light.[28]

In the quietness of this moment, you and I come to a fork in our road of life. We must make a choice to "love" either darkness or Light. Which of the two roads will you take? My choice is to love the Light—may you choose to do so too!

---

27. John 1:5, 9, NIV.
28. John 3:19, NIV.

"I seek refuge in God from the intermeddling and mischief of cursed Satan." (Salah, "Ta'awwudh).

9

The Great War Behind All Wars: Satan's Hatred Against Allah

When the patriarch Jacob (Ya'coub), the son of Isaac (Ishaq), was fleeing alone from home, he lay down to sleep one night as a weary pilgrim in a dangerous place, and his heart was oppressed by a sense of fear and guilt. The gracious God gave him a dream which came as a wonderful breakthrough into his human understanding. He was not alone!

As he lay sleeping on the ground at Bethel with a stone for a pillow, he saw a ladder stretching from where he was, up to heaven, and there were angels ascending and descending on it.[1] Thus for the first time in his life Jacob saw beyond the shadows of this world into the reality of heaven's nearness to us. These angels are constantly working for believers, taking their prayers up to heaven and bringing back gracious answers. Without divine revelation, we could never know what is going on, and we would miss out on the fantastic blessings that lie unseen all around us. This ladder connects heaven above with the believer below.

---

1. Genesis 28:10-22.

The war behind all wars is the attempt of Iblis (Satan) to cut that ladder from heaven to earth so that the world is left in darkness and loneliness. Those who are thus cut off are aptly described as "aliens, ... and strangers from the covenants of promise, having no hope, and without God in the world."[2] Satan cannot actually cut the ladder itself; but he can throw a cloud of darkness over the truth, so that for the world the ladder might just as well not be there.

This Satan (Iblis) is described in the honoured Qur'an as the angel who "was puffed up with pride, and became of the number of unbelievers."[3] He falsely accused Allah, saying, "Thou hast seduced me." His hatred of Allah led him to say that he would fight a war against him: "I will surely tempt them to disobedience in the earth, and I will seduce such of them as shall be thy chosen servants."[4] It is he who has "sown discord between ... brethren."[5]

No intelligent person can doubt that there is a Satan, the source and continuer of evil in the earth. There is no evil in Allah, "Lord of the worlds, the Beneficent, the Merciful."[6] Although Allah is the Almighty One, he does have an enemy who will oppose him until the final Day of Judgment.

Man needs to understand the nature of this great conflict between Satan and Allah, and how the evil angels of Satan (evil *jinns*) work to foment trouble in the earth. It is impossible to have a clear understanding of life today without grasping the reality of this great war behind all wars, for this invisible conflict vitally affects every human being living on planet earth.

This mysterious war actually began in heaven, for it was there that Satan's hatred against Allah was first brought out in

---

2. Ephesians 2:12.
3. *The Qur'an*, 2:34, 7:11, 12.
4. *The Qur'an*, 15:31-40
5. *The Qur'an*, 12:5, 100.
6. *The Qur'an*, "The Fatihah."

the open. We find the story of the rebellion of Satan in this inspired vision:

> And there was war in heaven. Michael and his angels fought against the dragon, and the dragon and his angels fought back. But he was not strong enough, and they lost their place in heaven. The great dragon was hurled down—that ancient serpent called the devil or Satan, who leads the whole world astray. He was hurled to the earth, and his angels with him. Then I heard a loud voice in heaven say: "Now have come the salvation and the power and the kingdom of our God. ... For the accuser of our brothers, who accuses them before our God day and night, has been hurled down.[7]

The name Michael means "Who is like God?"[8] This raises a question: Why does the Sacred Record not simply say that Satan fought against God? Can anyone be *like* God? There is only *one* God! Here we face a profound mystery of the divine revelation. The one true Allah is greater and more glorious than our poor, finite, mortal minds can grasp. The holy, invisible Allah, disclosed himself in a manifestation of himself that Satan warred against.

Satan actually staged an attempted coup against God's government, and although he was not strong enough to overthrow him and usurp his place, Satan did succeed in getting one-third of the angels to join him.[9] The holy prophet Ezekiel (Shul-Kifl) was given a view of Satan's history under the symbol of the "king of Tyre," a man who tried to copy Satan:

> You were the model of perfection,
>   full of wisdom and perfect in beauty.
> You were in Eden,
>   the garden of God, ...

---

7. Revelation 12:7-10, NIV.
8. Compare Daniel 12:1, Jude 9, 1 Thessalonians 4:16, 17.
9. See Revelation 12:4.

> You were anointed as a guardian cherub,
>   for so I ordained you.
> You were on the holy mount of God;
>   you walked among the fiery stones.
> You were blameless in your ways
>   from the day you were created
>   till wickedness was found in you. ...
> You sinned. ...
> Your heart became proud
>   on account of your beauty,
> And you corrupted your wisdom
>   because of your splendor.
> So I threw you to the earth.[10]

Allah is too good to create someone like Satan as an enemy for us. He created a pure and holy angel whose name was Lucifer, or "Morning Star," and who was "blameless" until he himself invented the idea of rebellion against God:

> How you have fallen from heaven,
>   O morning star, son of the dawn!
> You have been cast down to the earth. ...
> You said in your heart,
>   "I will ascend to heaven;
> I will raise my throne
>   above the stars of God; ...
> I will make myself like the Most High."[11]

Many have had the idea that Iblis will never die. They have assumed that evil will continue forever, supposing that there is a kind of eternal "dualism" in Allah's universe (that both good and evil are needed to balance each other). Their idea is that although pure evil is bad, pure good is *too* good!

---

10. Ezekiel 28:12-17, NIV.
11. Isaiah 14:12-14, NIV.

There must, therefore, be a good Allah teamed up with a bad Devil who always keeps a kind of war going forever. This idea is not true.

Satan wants people to think this, because it puts Allah in a bad light. It makes it seem that he is too weak to conquer the problem of evil, and that, of course, means that evil is too strong for God. So he and Satan strike a kind of bargain between them, each to co-exist with the other, just as good people and bad people have to co-exist in this less-than-perfect world we live in.

Some even think that Satan is a member of Allah's staff, employed by him as the "manager" of his hell-fire department. Traditional pagan religions tend to regard evil as something which is eternally entrenched in the world—probably the real reason why corruption everywhere seems to be impossible to eradicate!

The inspired Word of Allah proclaims the good news that there will be a total eradication of Satan, sin, and evil in the future. To know and understand this good news is like having a light on a dark and stormy night when you must travel a road you've never been on before, a road upon which there are evil people or wild animals that you fear.

One of the companions of the Messiah, Simon Peter son of Jona, was impressed with the way the Holy Scriptures give assurance to the heart of man. In a general letter to believers, he said: "We are even more confident of the message proclaimed by the prophets. You will do well to pay attention to it, because it is like a lamp shining in a dark place until the Day dawns."[12] Many, many people are deeply worried; you can see unhappy faces everywhere. To know the good news that Satan is defeated will lift a heavy burden from many perplexed hearts.

---

12. 2 Peter 1:19, TEV.

The war that Satan began in heaven has been continued on earth. This enemy deceived our first parents and persuaded them to invite him in. They had been created noble, pure, and happy, having "dominion" over "every living thing that moveth upon the earth." They were made "in the image of God, ... male and female."[13] Adam was appointed Khalifa on earth.

Unfortunately, they invited Satan in because he promised them liberty in the "knowledge of good and evil," and aroused them to doubt the love and faithfulness of Allah.[14] Before they yielded to Satan's temptation, however, they had been honoured with this glorious "dominion":

> What is man, that thou art mindful of him? ... thou madest him to have dominion over the works of thy hands; thou hast put all things under his feet: all sheep and oxen, yea, and the beasts of the field; the fowl of the air, and the fish of the sea.[15]

It is clear for everyone to see that we have lost this "dominion"! Except for a few domesticated animals such as horses, camels and cattle, nature is *not* under our "dominion" at all. Lightning, storms, floods, earthquakes, are uncontrollable even by the scientists' most sophisticated inventions. Even the birds fly away from us! What has caused this loss of "dominion"? Our first parents wanted something higher than they had been created to have. Satan tempted them to aspire to be "as gods," and they chose to share his ambition to be "like the most High."[16] This was the deep sin that caused their fall; they expressed it outwardly in the open act of disobedience, reaching out to pluck the forbidden fruit and eat it.[17] This sin was more than a mere act of outward disobedience; it involved Satan's heart, and man's heart as well.

---

13. Genesis 1:26-28.
14. Genesis 2:16, 17; 3:4, 5.
15. Psalm 8:4-8.
16. Genesis 3:5; Isaiah 14:14.
17. Genesis 3:6; *The Qur'an*, 2; 7:20-22; 20:120, 121.

Sin is not merely a taboo, the doing of an act that Allah has arbitrarily prohibited; it is the cherished doubt of God's character of love, which leads to the desire to rise higher than our created position under him. There is, and can always be, only *one* Allah, therefore for Satan or man to desire to be "like the most High" requires that we push him off his high and holy throne and take his place. This was Satan's ambition in his attempted coup; and when he persuaded man to join him, he brought sin and evil into the world. "Sin entered the world through one man [Adam], and death through sin, and in this way death came to all men, because all sinned." [18]

There is no other explanation of why death is universal! A proud, unbelieving person will not wish to acknowledge this sober truth that Allah's Word discloses, but the world is too full of evil, suffering and death for anyone to successfully deny that sin is the cause of it all. Satan's principle of self-seeking, selfishness, and rebellion against Allah is everywhere. "The carnal mind is enmity against God." [19] This "enmity" is deeply ingrained within us, because the prophet Jeremiah wisely says, "The heart is deceitful above all things and beyond cure. Who can understand it?" [20] Sin deceives us, so that we cannot even understand ourselves, except in the light of Allah's revelation.

Since "enmity" is like a seed planted, what kind of fruit does it produce? If it is allowed to germinate in a human heart, take root and grow, everyone knows well what the fruit will be: murder or the attempt to murder. It is true that many people hate others and yet do not actually pull a trigger or poison them; and the reason is that their "enmity" is mercifully restrained by the good Spirit of God in one way or another.

---

18. Romans 5:12, NIV.
19. Romans 8:7.
20. Jeremiah 17:9, NIV.

If that divine restraint is removed, murder always follows because "whosoever hateth his brother *is* a murderer."[21] The desire becomes father to the deed.

Throughout long ages, the enemy, Satan, has brought misery, sickness, hatred, wars, corruption, death, into this fair earth. He caused persecution, especially against the true worshippers of Allah, trying to wipe them from the earth. Fortunately, he could not succeed, for Allah protected his faithful believers who were always as "strangers and pilgrims" in an alien world.[22]

Allah counted Satan's enmity and persecution as directed against *himself*. In fact, Satan's enmity *is* primarily directed against God, not man. His persecution of Allah's worshippers is an effort to persecute God in the same way that a man's enemy may attempt to get at him by harming his children. Allah's love for his faithful worshipers in an alien world is like that of a father for his children: "Like as a father pitieth his children, so the Lord pitieth them that fear him."[23]

Satan's fierce hatred against Allah was yet to find a target. When our first parents invited Satan in as "the prince of this world,"[24] Allah told them of the results of their sin, but he did not leave them to their ruin. He immediately showed them another facet of his divine character—that of being a Deliverer, Redeemer, and Saviour. This aspect of himself had not been known before, because sin had not yet entered his world.

In addition, therefore, to being our Creator, our Father, and our God, he must become our Saviour too, or he will deny his own attributes as "Lord of the worlds, the Beneficent, the Merciful" One.

---

21. 1 John 3:15, emphasis supplied.
22. See Hebrews 11:13.
23. Psalm 103:13.
24. See John 14:30.

Allah wanted our first parents to hear the good news of his redemptive work as a Saviour, and to them he outlined the future war behind all wars. This revelation is in what he said to Satan:

> I will put enmity
>   between you and the woman,
>   and between your offspring and hers;
> he will crush your head,
>   and you will strike his heel.[25]

The woman's "offspring" is the long-awaited Messiah, through whom Allah would redeem man's lost "dominion" from the usurper, Satan. The great war would intensify until it became a death-grapple between Allah and Satan, for Satan would "strike his heel," but the Messiah would *crush his head*. In other words, the Messiah would be wounded in the great war, but Satan would be *mortally* wounded and would eventually be utterly defeated and die the "second death."[26]

It is clear in the honoured Qur'an that Hazrat Abraham understood the essential features of this great conflict, for it was no doubt he who passed on the details of our first parents' mistake to the later prophets, including the prophet Moses (Musa). In Allah's provision of a "tremendous Victim" to ransom his son, Abraham saw and understood the principle of *redemption by substitute* so necessary in Allah's plan to defeat Satan forever.[27]

Since "whosoever hateth his brother is a murderer,"[28] it is hardly surprising that Satan's hatred of God was manifested in his attempt to murder the Messiah. It was in that desire to murder, that Satan would in fact defeat himself. He would over-reach himself, captive to his own evil impulses.

---

25. Genesis 3:15, NIV.
26. See Revelation 20:14.
27. *The Qur'an*, 37:107.
28. 1 John 3:15.

Allah was too great and too wise to destroy Satan in the beginning, for such an act would not have been understood by angels or his servants in the world and throughout the universe. Allah must patiently permit Satan to develop his malicious purposes, until it was plain for everyone to see that his new "invention" of sin is actually an attempt to displace Allah from his throne and murder him. Satan needed time to demonstrate this. Allah must not allow secret doubts to exist among his worship pers. Only by allowing the evil character of Satan to be fully revealed could the great war finally be won.

This is the reason why Allah instituted the ancient system of blood sacrifices. They revealed two important truths that his worshipers must understand: (a) Satan's enmity against Allah would at last be brought out in the open by his attempt to murder the Messiah; (b) at the same time, Allah would redeem sinful man by his "tremendous Victim,"[29] for all the ancient prophets, instructed by Allah, clearly saw that "without shedding of blood there is no remission" of sins.[30] This was the truth that Abraham understood when Allah provided that substitute to die in place of his son.

In the beginning, Satan envied Adam because Allah had appointed him Khalifa, vicegerent, on this earth. Sadly, Adam foolishly listened to Satan, thus giving him an advantage. Satan's purpose has been to wrest from Adam that honoured position of Khalifa, and the tragic evil that for thousands of years has brought sorrow and tears to so many on earth is evidence enough of his efforts. Allah's divine plan of redemption is one of infinite wisdom: the long-awaited Messiah must wrest from Satan this usurped honour of Khalifa in order to restore it to man.

Now we have come to the time when the great battle of

---

29. *The Qur'an*, 37:107.
30. Hebrews 9:22.

the ages is to be concluded. In the inspired vision which the prophet John saw, Satan fights desperately just before the end of the world, "because he knoweth that he hath but a short time. ... And the dragon was wroth with the woman [the believing "offspring"] and went to make war with the remnant of her seed, which keep the commandments of God."[31]

Allah will win the war of the ages! "Praise be to Allah, Lord of the worlds, the Beneficent, the Merciful, Owner of the Day of Judgment."[32]

---

31. Revelation 12:12, 17.
32. *The Qur'an*, "The Fatihah."

"And afterwards We inspired thee: Follow the religion of Abraham, as one by nature upright. He was not of the idolaters." (*The Qur'an*, 16:123).

10

Why Allah Commanded Hazrat Abraham to Offer His Son

Millions of believers consider Hazrat Abraham to be their "father." This is the greatest honour that could ever come to a mortal man, but it was necessary for Allah to test his faith carefully. His life story is an example to us, for our own human experience is encapsulated in his fantastic struggle with doubt and despair. For us to "follow the religion of Abraham" requires that we understand his experience.

One of Abraham's descendants, the apostle Paul, was especially inspired by his faith. In the letters which he wrote to fellow-believers he appealed to them to have a faith like that of Abraham. One letter, written to the church at Rome, described the faith of Abraham as "who against hope, believed in hope."[1] This refers to the fact that for many years he hoped for a son, according to Allah's promise, when really there seemed to be no human hope because both he and his wife were too old. The struggle to believe went on for decades, long after most people would have given up their faith in God.

---

1. Romans 4:18.

Allah's promise was, "Your wife Sarah will bear you a son and you will name him Isaac." "Abraham bowed down with his face touching the ground, but he began to laugh when he thought, 'Can a man have a child when he is a hundred years old? Can Sarah have a child at ninety?'"

Abraham had a son by the Egyptian girl Hagar. This son, Ishmael, was blessed by God. He had twelve sons, each of which became a prince of a nation. When God promised the birth of Isaac by Sarah, he added:

> "'I have heard your request about Ishmael, so I will bless him and give him many children and many descendants. ... I will make a great nation of his descendants. But I will keep my covenant with your son Isaac, who will be born to Sarah about this time next year.'" [2]

The honoured Qur'an says:

> His [Abraham's] wife Sarah was standing by, and she laughed; and We promised her Isaac, and after Isaac, Jacob. She said, Alas! shall I bear a son, who am old; this my husband also being advanced in years? Verily this would be a wonderful thing.[3]

The lesson of faith was impressed on Abraham's heart: when Allah makes a promise, *he* is the one to keep it; Abraham's own works are of no merit. He must not think of himself as in any sense equal with Allah. The covenant which Allah made with Abraham is his *promise* to Abraham, and he expects no promise in return—all he asks is faith to believe *his* promise.

After the great Flood of Noah, we read that Allah made a covenant with the birds and the beasts,[4] but Allah did not ask the birds and animals to promise him anything! Our human covenants consist of two parties making mutual promises.

---

2. Genesis 17:15-21, TEV.
3. "Hud," surah 11.
4. Genesis 9:9.

Allah's covenant is his promise alone, and man's part is to *believe* it. This was the lesson that Allah must impress upon Abraham, so he can truly be the "father of the faithful," that is, of those who are "full" of faith.

To help Abraham remember that righteousness comes by faith and not by works, Allah gave him the significant sign of circumcision. He intended a great truth to be taught by this sign: the new spiritual life does not come "of the will of the flesh, nor of the will of man, but of God."[5] Abraham was circumcised, at the age of 99. "By faith" he was able to make Sarah pregnant, and at the age of 90 she bore him his son Isaac. Isaac was therefore called "the child of promise."[6]

Everybody for a great distance around was talking about the miracle: a woman of 90 years of age gave birth to a baby! Abraham and Sarah understood the lesson: Allah's "covenant" is a one-sided thing; and since it is his promise, *he* will fulfil it. As Isaac was the fruit of their faith *together* in their one-flesh union as husband and wife, so righteousness is the fruit of man's faith in Allah's covenant, and not the fruit of his own meritorious works. This is the heart of true religion, for it alone glorifies Allah.

When Allah repeated the promise to Abraham, "It is through Isaac that you will have the descendants I have promised,"[7] he did not mean that Isaac's *literal* descendants should *automatically* have priority over Ishmael's; they were both sons of Abraham. Allah must be fair. His blessings are not arbitrarily given, but are bestowed on condition of faith. This silences all charges of injustice.

The great mistake of the Jews has been to imagine that they are special merely because they trace their *genetic* descent

---

5. John 1:13.
6. Galatians 4:28.
7. Genesis 21:12, TEV.

through Isaac. All who have true faith in Allah and worship him alone are the *true* descendants of Abraham, and like Isaac are "children of the promise." If only the Jews had understood that Abraham is the "father of the faithful," that is, those "full of faith," how much war and bloodshed on this sad earth would never have taken place! What Allah values is the heart and the character, not the fleshly pedigree which leads to pride and arrogance, and even cruelty toward other people.

The Jews never understood that circumcision was a "sign" or "seal" of righteousness by faith, but they took it to be a merit or work that *commended* them to Allah—actually a form of idolatry itself! While they derided those who bowed down to images, they unconsciously made an idol of, and worshipped, their own circumcision. What blindness! Most of them completely missed the lesson Allah had taught Abraham, although there have always been a few Jews who were true "children of the promise" by faith.

But Allah had still another lesson that he must impress on Hazrat Abraham. When he was 120 years old, Allah gave him the greatest test of all. His love for his son was tender and deep, and Allah tried his faith with the most difficult command any mortal man has had to obey. He awakened Abraham one night and commanded him to take his beloved son to a certain mountain and offer him there as a sacrifice!

The problem the honoured patriarch had to wrestle with was this: *why* would Allah make such a command? The heathen gods of the Canaanites demanded such sacrifices; was the one true Allah as bad as they? Where was his love? Could Abraham continue to believe in Allah when everything *seemed* to indicate that he was as cruel as these heathen gods? Could he have known that Christ's apostle, John, would later say that Allah *is* "love"?[8]

---

8. 1 John 4:8.

Abraham awakened his sleeping son in the darkness and whispered the command to get up and go on a journey with him. Their trip took three days, and Abraham's heart was heavy. Each night he prayed for some change in Allah's will, but no command came to change what Abraham had heard at first. Finally on the third day he sighted the mountain on which the sacrifice should be made.

He told the servants: "Stay here with the donkey. The boy and I will go over there and worship, and then we will come back to you."[9] It was only natural that the boy should wonder where the animal for the sacrifice was!

"Father!"

"Yes, my son?"

"I see that you have the coals and the wood, but where is the lamb for the sacrifice?"

He replied that Allah would provide one, and the two of them walked on together.

"Abraham built an altar and arranged the wood on it." Then he told his son what Allah had commanded. Can you imagine the horror that his son felt? He was young and strong, and could easily have overpowered his aged father and run away; but as his father explained it all, the boy decided to share his father's faith. He willingly submitted—the most amazing devotion of any boy! The father's faith and devotion were perfectly reflected or equalled by the son's. The father so loved that he gave his son, and the son so loved that he gave himself!

The world had never seen such a demonstration of love, such whole-hearted devotion to God on the part of both a human father and son. Here was an impressive and deeply significant picture of God's love for a wayward world.

Father and son embrace in a last good-bye, their hearts bleeding with sorrow. Abraham ties the lad, lays him on the

---

9. Genesis 22:5.

altar, and grasps the knife, raising it in obedience to Allah's command to slay his beloved son.

> Suddenly, God called out from heaven: "'Abraham! Abraham!'"
> He answered, "'Yes, here I am.'"
> "'Don't hurt the boy or do anything to him. ... Now I know that you fear [have obedient reverence for] God, because you have not kept back your only son from him.'" [10]

Abraham looked around and saw a ram caught in a bush by its horns. He went and took it and offered it as a burnt offering in the place of his son. Then he named that sacred place, "Allah Provides." In the original language there are two names for God, each of which reveals a different aspect of his glorious, divine character. What Allah (El) *demands* of Abraham, the LORD *gives*. It is the one true Allah who does both—who *demands* and then *gives*.

Why did Allah give that blood sacrifice? Here is the point of the great story. The honoured Qur'an says of Abraham's son: "We ransomed him with a tremendous Victim.[11] Many commemorate this great "ransom" with the Feast of El-Adha, when they kill a sheep symbolizing Abraham's offering up of his son. This sacrifice of Abraham has made a great impression on millions of minds around the world. Allah is seeking to teach us a lesson.

The first blood sacrifice was offered by Allah himself when he killed an innocent animal in order to provide a clothing of skins to cover the nakedness of Adam. "Unto Adam also and to his wife did the Lord God make coats of skins, and clothed them." [12]

---

10. Genesis 22:6-14, TEV.
11. The Qur'an, 37:107.
12. Genesis 3:21.

Then there was the second instance of the offering of a blood sacrifice, this time by Abel. Adam's two sons, Cain and Abel, brought different kinds of offerings. Cain brought his own "works," the fruit he had gathered from his garden, but Allah would not accept his offering because it contained no blood symbolizing the death of an innocent creature. No one can "buy" the favour of Allah. A whole train-load of fruit and vegetables would not obtain forgiveness for even one sin. Cain was making a mistake when he tried to fulfil Allah's covenant of promise by his own planning and works.

Abel was wise. He did not bring his own works; instead he "brought the first lamb born to one of his sheep, killed it, and gave the best parts of it as an offering." We read that Allah "was pleased with Abel and his offering." [13]

Why?

For the same reason that he gave "a tremendous Victim" to take the place of Abraham's son. Those innocent animals died as a symbolic substitute for Abel and Abraham's son, who were both "ransomed" from death. A ransom is something paid in order to save someone's life. The "tremendous Victim" was not something that Abraham provided—*God* gave it. This was the important lesson that all blood sacrifices were intended to teach!

There is no way that a ram caught in a thicket could be called" a tremendous Victim" by comparison with the precious son of Abraham. A ram is absolutely nothing in comparison with a human being, especially the son of Abraham. How could Allah compare the blood of an animal with that of his "friend's" son?

Animals' blood was, of itself, useless in sacrifice to God. The prophet Micah said wisely:

---

13. Genesis 4:1-5, TEV; The Qur'an, 5:27.

> What shall I bring to the Lord, the God of heaven, when I come to worship him? Shall I bring the best calves to burn as offerings to him? Will the Lord be pleased if I bring him thousands of sheep or endless streams of olive oil? Shall I offer him my first-born child to pay for my sins?[14]

No, Allah said, for "the blood of bulls and goats can never take away sins."[15] Animals' "flesh and their blood reacheth not unto Allah, but the devotion from you reacheth Him."[16] When David (Daud) committed adultery, and then murder to try to cover it up, he prayed: "You do not want sacrifices, or I would offer them; you are not pleased with burnt-offerings. My sacrifice is a humble spirit, O God; you will not reject a humble and repentant heart."[17] The Jews missed the point, for he said to them through his prophet Amos:

> I hate your religious festivals; I cannot stand them! When you bring me burnt-offerings and grain-offerings, I will not accept them; I will not accept the animals you have fattened to bring me as offerings.[18]

Then why did Allah institute the system of blood sacrifices? They were only to be a "shadow" of the truly "tremendous Victim" who was to ransom the human race by his blood. He is called the "Lamb that was slain from the foundation of the world."[19] Abel's blood sacrifice could not truly ransom his soul, but the innocent animal he offered prefigured "the Lamb of God, which taketh away the sin of the world."[20] By offering a blood sacrifice, Abel confessed his faith in that true divine sacrifice, the ultimate reality prefigured by all blood sacrifices.

---

14. Micah 6:6, 7.
15. Hebrews 10:4.
16. *The Qur'an*, 22:37.
17. Psalm 51:16, 17, TEV.
18. Amos 5:21, 22, TEV.
19. Revelation 13:8.
20. John 1:29.

When Abraham offered the ram that Allah had gave on Mount Moriah, he also confessed his faith in that "tremendous Victim." Allah was not pleased with the animal's blood; he was pleased with Abraham's faith in the Lamb of God, the divinely provided sacrifice for the sins of the world, whose blood has true power to cleanse from the stain of sin.

Why is this so? Simply because sin is a state of "enmity against God," of alienation from him; and a reconciliation must take place so that the estranged human heart is "at-one" with God again. There is no way that this great reconciliation could ever take place, except by the sacrifice of a sinless life to atone for the breaking of Allah's holy law.

There is a link that binds Abraham on Mount Moriah (where the Al Aqsa Mosque now stands) with the sacrifice of the Lamb of God. Think of a father willing to sacrifice his beloved son! What tremendous faith Abraham had! Jesus (Issa) said to the Jews, "Your father Abraham rejoiced at the thought of seeing my day; he saw it and was glad." [21] Abraham was a true prophet and could see things that ordinary people could not see. How did he "see" Jesus' day? How could he actually "see" him 1,900 years before Jesus was born of the virgin Mary?

Allah permitted his "friend", Abraham, to go through an experience that helped him appreciate Allah's true character. The best good news that the world has ever heard, is also the heart of the Holy Injil: "God so loved the world that he gave his one and only Son, that whoever believes in him shall not perish but have eternal life." [22] (The words "one and only Son" do not mean that God slept with some woman and sired a son as humans do. Neither Jesus nor any true follower of his has ever suggested such a thought. The original term is *monogenes*, from *monos*, "only," and *genos*, "kind" and it refers to the "only

---

21. John 8:56, NIV.
22. John 3:16, NIV.

one of a kind." The expression describes someone who is as dear and beloved as Abraham's son was to him.)

When Allah made this great sacrifice, he was not helped with a substitute as Abraham was, for there was no one else who could be given as an offering for the sins of the world.[23] Allah is *not* like the terrible Canaanite gods who demanded the sacrifice of children; he would not permit Abraham to actually offer *his* son; nor was he pleased to see Jesus suffer on the cross. God is not a heathen deity who must be placated or appeased by human sacrifices!

Then why did he permit Jesus to suffer so? We can ask another question, closely related: why did he ask his friend, Abraham, to live through the terrible agony of the three-day journey, going right up to the very point of lifting the knife up to heaven, ready to bring it down to pierce the heart of his beloved son? Why must Abraham be permitted to suffer so? Is that the way to treat your "friend"?

Abraham must not be excused from enduring his great trial, because he must "see" how great is the love of Allah for a lost world plunged into sin and misery. No one can be a "friend" of God unless he understands the heart of God, for Abraham was more than a mere slave crawling on his belly before Allah. You remember how Allah respected Abraham concerning the destruction of Sodom and Gomorrah. He said, "Shall I hide from Abraham what I am about to do? Abraham will surely become a great and powerful nation, and all nations on earth will be blessed through him. For I have chosen him, so that he will direct his children and his household after him to keep the way of the Lord by doing what is right and just."[24]

Then Allah shared the full plan to destroy those wicked cities in the plain with his "friend," and he permitted Abraham

---

23. See Romans 3:24-26.
24. Genesis 18:17-19, NIV.

to plead and reason with him in the same way that two friends would talk and reason together. In order to be the "father of the faithful," Abraham must be permitted, as far as is possible for a mortal man, to share the heart of God: his feelings and his purposes. Abraham must appreciate Allah's infinite justice and love. This is why he must climb Mount Moriah and go through an experience that no other father has ever been called to go through. He must go through the experience of "sacrificing" the one nearest and dearest to him, so that as "father of the faithful" he can teach the world to appreciate how Allah loves us so much that he *too* gave the one nearest and dearest to himself.

The world is plunging into ruin. Man cannot save himself. Nations, civilizations, cultures, are mad with hatred and corruption. Immorality, pornography, crime, and drug and alcohol abuse, are ruining the quality of human life, while cruel and bloody war is increasingly resorted to as a means of settling quarrels. Hopeful people who have expected great human progress are frankly worried about tomorrow. Around the world, rich and poor alike are becoming increasingly godless and corrupt. Allah knows all about this, and although true believers in him are the special objects of his care, he loves all the people of the world, not just a little elite group of special ones.

Abraham "saw" Jesus' day because he could appreciate the love of God for this world as being like the love of a father for his dear son, and yet a love that led him to make this ultimate sacrifice for the redemption of the world. In our next chapter we must look deeper into this great truth.

"Jesus spake, Lo, I am the slave of Allah. He hath given me the Scripture and hath appointed me a prophet and hath made me blessed wheresoever I may be and hath enjoined upon me prayer and almsgiving so long as I remain alive. Peace on me the day I was born and the day I die and the day I shall be raised alive."

(*The Qur'an*, **19:30-33**).

11

Who Is Jesus Christ (Sayyidna Al Masih)?

The Holy Injil tells us that Abraham anticipated the day of Jesus, in that he looked forward to it. He well understood that no animal blood could redeem his son from death, for only a "tremendous Victim" could do that. How did Abraham look forward to the coming of Jesus?

The enemies of Jesus (Issa) were unfair and false when they accused him of trying to make himself God he never claimed to do such a thing. Man cannot make himself to be God! What Jesus *did* claim was that God had condescended to reveal himself in a man. The movement was not from earth up to heaven, but from heaven down to earth. We cannot find fault with Allah's loving revelation of himself, proceeding from heaven to earth. Would not finding fault be blasphemy?

Jesus asked a question of the Jews: "'What do you think about the Christ? Whose son is he?'" He asks us the same question. Was he a liar or did he tell the truth? This is a supremely important question, for we cannot get the problems of life straightened out until we answer it correctly.

Jesus will return again, and we shall all see him. Our standing then will depend on the answer we give to this honest question now.

The honoured Qur'an teaches us to expect the second coming of Jesus in power and glory (see chapter 13 of this book). Why will Allah send him again? Would it not seem more reasonable and appropriate for him to send the prophet of Islam a second time? No, we find that it will be Jesus who will be sent the second time. What is the reason for this very special honour to be shown to Jesus?

Consider the many unique aspects of his nature, his character, and his life:

1. *Jesus' birth was different to that of any other human being.* He had no earthly father. We read in the honoured Qur'an that Jesus was born of a virgin: "O, Mary! Lo, Allah gives you glad tidings of a Word from Him, whose name is the Messiah, Jesus son of Mary." Mary replied: "How shall I have a son, since a man hath not touched me?" The angel said, "So God createth that which He pleaseth: when He decreeth a thing, He only saith unto it, Be, and it is."[1]

Jesus was born by the power of God, as the prophet Isaiah had said 700 years before: "The Lord himself will give you a sign: the virgin will be with child and will give birth to a son, and will call him Immanuel."[2] The Hebrew word does not necessarily mean "virgin," but the apostle Matthew quoted it as "virgin." The scholars who translated Isaiah into Greek more than a century before Christ used *parthenos*, the word for "virgin." In the Qur'an, Jesus is referred to as Issa ibn Maryam, Jesus the son of Mary. Abdullah al-Baidawi, the classical commentator on the Qur'an, recognizes the Semitic practice of calling a man as the son of his mother only when his father is unknown. He also recognizes that in Islam Jesus

---

1. *The Qur'an*, 3:44-46.
2. Isaiah 7:14, NIV.

is regarded as the Son of the Virgin Mary, who was begotten by the creative Word of God.³

The word "Immanuel" means "Allah with us." The Injil tells us how Isaiah's prophecy was fulfilled:

> This is how the birth of Jesus Christ came about. His mother Mary was pledged to be married to Joseph, but before they came together, she was found to be with child through the Holy Spirit. ... An angel of the Lord appeared to him [Joseph] in a dream and said, "Joseph, son of David, do not be afraid to take Mary home as your wife because what is conceived in her is from the Holy Spirit. She will give birth to a son, and you are to give him the name Jesus, because he will save his people from their sins."
>
> All this took place to fulfill what the Lord had said through the prophet: "The virgin will be with child and will give birth to a son, and they will call him Immanuel"—which means, "God with us."
>
> When Joseph woke up, he did what the angel of the Lord had commanded him and took Mary home as his Wife. But he had no union with her until she gave birth to a son. And he gave him the name Jesus.⁴

We are all "children born ... of natural descent, ... of ... a husband's will."⁵ Jesus, however, was different. He is called *al Manzul*—he who descended. How can this be?

The first words of the Holy Bible say: "In the beginning God created the heavens and the earth, ... and the Spirit of God was hovering over the waters. And God said, 'Let there be light,' and there was light."⁶ Three names of one God are disclosed here: (a) Allah; (b) the Spirit of Allah; and (c) the Word of Allah. The Injil says, of Jesus:

---

3. Ethlebert Stauffer, *Jesus and His Story*, translated by Richard and Clara Winston, New York: Alfred A. Knopf, 1960.
4. Matthew 1:18-25, NIV.
5. John 1:13.
6. Genesis 1:1-3, NIV.

In the beginning was the Word, and the Word was with God and the Word was God. He was with God in the beginning. Through him all things were made; without him nothing was made that has been made. In him was life, and that life was the light of men. ... The Word became flesh and lived for a while among us.[7]

The honoured Qur'an reports the words of the angel to Mary: "Mary, God gives you good tidings of a word from him whose name is Messiah, Jesus, son of Mary; high honoured shall he be in this world and the next, near stationed to God. ... Righteous he shall be." (This name, ... A word from him," Kalimat Allah, is a clear description of Jesus.) We read further in the surah "Mary": "that is Jesus, son of Mary, the word of truth concerning which they are in doubt."[8]

A man's word expresses what he is and we can never know what a man is until he speaks that word. For if the word remains hidden in his mind, the man also remains hidden, even if we look at his outward appearance. If the man is open, loving, and honest, he will speak his word so that we can truly know him. The "word" is the disclosure, the unveiling, the revelation, of a person's character.

Allah is open, loving and honest. He is not hiding himself to deceive us, therefore he sent Jesus in this unique position of being his Word—to reveal himself to us, in language we could understand. That language was "Immanuel," "God with us."

Allah and the Spirit of Allah in the creation are one; in the same way Allah and the Word of Allah are one.

There is but one true God. The Scriptures do not teach the blasphemy of "three gods."

2. *The character of Jesus was a perfect demonstration of the active love of Allah.* No other man has ever equalled his character,

---

7. John 1:1-14, NIV.
8. *The Qur'an*, 3:44, 45, 19:34.

because no other man was declared by Allah to be his Word. He could say to his enemies: "Which of you can silence me by pointing out one sin that I have done?"[9] All other human beings have needed forgiveness: David asked for it; Abraham asked for it; but Jesus neither asked for nor needed forgiveness.

His closest companion, John the apostle, said: "In him is no sin,"[10] while his friend, Peter the apostle, said:

> "'He committed no sin, and no deceit was found in his mouth.'"[11]

The book of Hebrews adds that he was "tempted in every way, just as we are—yet was without sin."[12] What a witness—from those who knew him best!

3. *The words of Jesus were different from those of any prophet.* He had the gift of speaking in parables and telling stories that gripped the attention of his listeners, even his enemies. These parables are like a spring of water that is so crystal clear that you can see right to the bottom, and yet it is very deep. He told of a shepherd who went in search of one lost sheep, leaving the other 99 safe in the fold; he told of the lost boy who left home and spent all his inheritance on riotous living, yet was welcomed back by his loving father; he told of the woman who searched for her one lost silver coin. Each parable grips our human hearts as no other stories ever could.[13]

Once his enemies, the chief priests, sent soldiers to arrest him and bring him in for trial and condemnation.

The soldiers came to where he was speaking to the people. They listened, perhaps for hours. Finally they returned to the priests without him.

---

9. John 8:46, Arabic version.
10. 1 John 3:5.
11. 1 Peter 2:22, NIV.
12. Hebrews 4:15, NIV
13. See Luke 15:1-32.

"'Why didn't you bring him in?'"

"'No one ever spoke the way this man does,' the guards declared.'" [14]

Jesus was not content to tell people what to do. He said, "I have set you an example that you should do as I have done for you." "Whoever follows me will never walk in darkness, but will have the light of life." He said, "I am the light of the world."[15]

A wise old man once explained the relationship of Jesus to all prophets this way: he is like the sun, while they are like the moon which merely shines with reflected light. Moonlight is a wonderful thing and we are grateful for it in the darkness of night; but when the sun rises no one cares any longer for the moon. The prophet Malachi calls Jesus "the Sun of righteousness."[16] He never wanes as the moon does, and he shines on every human heart around the world as does the sun. Even the poorest man can have sunshine!

I was once a visitor in the city of Zurich Switzerland looking for a camping place. I asked a Swiss gentleman if he would kindly tell me how to find it. "No" he replied, "it will be better if I take you there." So he graciously took me all the way across that great city up and down hills, around drives and circles where I would have become hopelessly lost, until we arrived at the camping place. Jesus is not like a road-map telling us where to go; he says, *"I am the way."* [17]

4. *The names and titles of Jesus are unique.* He is called our Advocate, the Angel, the Archangel, the Branch, the Bridegroom, the Daystar, the Door, Immanuel, the Faithful and True, the Holy One, the I AM, the Just One, the King

---

14. John 7:32-46, NIV.
15. John 8:12; 9:5, NIV.
16. Malachi 4:2.
17. John 14:6.

of kings, the Lamb of God the Light of the world, the Lion of the tribe of Judah, the Man Child, the Messenger of the Covenant Michael ("Who is like God?"), the Prince of life, the Prince of Peace, the Rock, the Servant, the Saviour, the Good Shepherd, the Son of David, the Water of life, and many other names as well.

Allah said of him, "this is my beloved Son: hear him."[18] What did he mean when he said that? By saymg this he meant that Jesus is unique among all others, as a son is different from anyone else in the world. He did not teach polytheism, or that God had sexual relations with a woman to produce offspring. The Bible nowhere teaches such a thing. A son is the "image" or likeness of his father. Jesus said to his disciples, "He that hath seen me hath seen the Father."[19] This illustrates the relationship. Allah spoke through Jesus: "The Son is the radiance of God's glory and the exact representation of his being."[20]

Thus Jesus supersedes the prophets. They are known by their distinct titles; as Abraham the "friend of God" (Khalil Allah), or Moses the "spokesman with God" (Kalim Allah), but in the honoured Qur'an Jesus is called the "Spirit of God" (Ruh Allah).

5. *His power is unique.* The things he did are the same as what God does. Who can raise the dead, except God? Jesus raised the dead son of the widow of Nain, and Lazarus (a man who had been dead four days).[21] Who can cleanse lepers, except God? Jesus cleansed them.[22] He also opened the eyes of the blind.[23] No one was ever sent away from Jesus as incurable.

---

18. Luke 9:35.
19. John 14:9.
20. Hebrews1:3, NIV.
21. Luke 7:11-16, John 11:1-44.
22. Luke 5:12, 13.
23. John 9:1-7.

There is a difference between the way the ancient prophets healed the sick and the way that Jesus did it. They healed in the name of Allah; the Lord Jesus Christ healed them in his own name.

On one occasion, the Jews, opposing him as usual, said, " 'Why does this fellow talk like that? He's blaspheming! Who can forgive sins but God alone?'

"Immediately Jesus knew in his spirit that this was what they were thinking in their hearts, and he said to them, 'Why are you thinking these things? Which is easier: to say to the paralytic, "Your sins are forgiven," or to say, "Get up, take your mat and walk?" But that you may know that the Son of Man has authority on earth to forgive sins,' ... He said to the paralytic, '*I tell you*, get up, take your mat and go home.' He got up, took his mat, and walked out in full view of them all. This amazed everyone and they praised God, saying, 'We have never seen anything like this!'" [24]

When he resurrected Lazarus, he came to the door of the tomb and called out, "Lazarus, come forth", and Lazarus awoke from death and came forth. On this occasion Jesus said, "I am the resurrection, and the life." [25] He is the only hope anyone has of a resurrection from the dead, for all who are now in their graves patiently await hearing his voice. Jesus says: "As the Father hath life in himself; so hath he given to the Son to have life in himself .... Marvel not at this: for the hour is coming, in the which all that are in the graves shall hear his voice, and shall come forth; they that have done good, unto the resurrection of life; and they that have done evil, unto the resurrection of damnation." [26] You and I will be among those who will face him.

---

24. Mark 2:6-12, NIV, emphasis supplied.
25. John 11:43, 25, NIV.
26. John 5:26-29.

As he had power to give life to the dead, so now he has power to give new life to all who will come to him. His business is transforming hearts and lives.

6. *His victory over death is the only hope the world has.* The prophets foretold his sufferings long before he was born in Bethlehem. Isaiah said of him 700 years earlier:

> He was pierced for our transgressions,
>   he was crushed for our iniquities;
> the punishment that brought us peace was upon him,
>   and by his wounds we are healed. ...
> the Lord has laid on him the iniquity of us all. ...
>
> By oppression and judgment, he was taken away.
>   And who can speak of his descendants?
> For he was cut off from the land of the living;
>   for the transgression of my people he was stricken.
> He was assigned a grave with the wicked,
>   and with the rich in his death,
> though he had done no violence,
>   nor was any deceit in his mouth. ...
>
> The Lord makes his life a guilt offering. ...
>
> He poured out his life unto death,
>   and was numbered with the transgressors.
> For he bore the sin of many.[27]

Daniel, 500 years before, predicted that a power inspired by Satan would' 'take his stand against the Prince of princes", and that "the Anointed One [the Christ] will be cut off."[28] He adds that the "Prince of the covenant" would "be broken."[29]

---

27. Isaiah 53:5-12, NIV; this text is confirmed by the Qumran scrolls as very ancient.
28. Daniel 8:25, 9:26, NIV.
29. Daniel 11:22.

Jesus Christ himself knew these Scriptures and told his disciples that he would suffer by "the elders and chief priests and scribes" at Jerusalem.[30] Which of us knows *where* he will die, whether at home or in a foreign land? Who of us can predict *when* he will die? Or *how*: of old age, or sickness, or an accident, or in war? The Lord Jesus knew and gave all the details of his own death.[31]

In the truest sense of the word, however, no one actually killed him, for no one had the power to do that. If he had chosen not to die, he would have been just as free to escape from his tormentors, as Abraham's healthy young son was free to flee from his aged father on Mt. Moriah, if he had chosen to do so. Jesus did not die as a martyr or as a genuine captive held against his will. He said: "I lay down my life—only to take it up again. No one takes it from me, but I lay it down of my own accord. I have authority to lay it down and authority to take it up again."[32]

Having never sinned, he was not compelled to die. At any moment he could have called for rescue from heaven, but he loves us, and suffered and submitted because he wanted to bear our guilt. Isaiah says of him:

"He was pierced for our transgressions, he was crushed for our iniquities; ... and by his wounds we are healed. ... The Lord has laid on him the iniquity of us all."[33]

Unlike any other man, he had power to take up his life again, and he did so on the third day. This was predicted by the holy prophets. David (Daud) said concerning him: "Thou wilt not leave my soul in hell [the grave]; neither wilt thou suffer thine Holy One to see corruption. Thou wilt show me the path of life."[34] Allah showed him that "path of life"

---

30. Matthew 16:21.
31. Luke 18:31-33.
32. John 10:17, 18, NIV.
33. Isaiah 53:5, 6.
34. Psalm 16:10, 11.

on his resurrection morning. The apostle Peter quoted these words of David and applied them to the resurrection of Jesus, because, he pointed out, they could not have been fulfilled concerning David, whose tomb was still with them.[35]

The Romans and the Jews did all they could to seal Jesus' tomb so that he would never come forth again. They had no doubt that he was dead when his disciples buried him, for as the Roman soldier pierced his side with a spear, streams of water and blood flowed forth, proving that he died of a ruptured heart.[36] (Even this was predicted by the prophet Zechariah.)[37]

For 40 days, the resurrected Jesus remained with his astonished followers, and was seen by 500 of them.[38] They ate with him and talked with him.

After 40 days were ended and his followers had had opportunity to see him and examine him, including the wounds in his hands, feet, and side, he was taken up into heaven "before their very eyes, and a cloud hid him from their sight." Allah highly exalted him, "to the highest place and gave him the name that is above every name, that at the name of Jesus every knee should bow, in heaven and on earth and under the earth, and every tongue confess that Jesus Christ is Lord."[39] Allah gave the highest place to the one who had poured out his soul unto death in order to ransom us as the "tremendous Victim."

7. *Jesus is now installed as our heavenly High Priest*. As his cross fulfilled the symbolic antitype of the ram offered in place of Abraham's son, so he fulfils by his heavenly work the antitypical role of the ancient High Priest. This "highest

---

35. Acts 2:25-29.
36. John 19:33-35.
37. Zechariah 12:10.
38. 1 Corinthians 15:3-7; Acts 1:1-3.
39. Acts 1:9-11; Philippians 2:9-11, NIV.

place" that Allah has given him is a place of continual service. Says the book of Hebrews: "We have a great high priest who has gone through the heavens, Jesus ... we do not have a high priest who is unable to sympathize with our weaknesses, but we have one who has been tempted in every way, just as we are—yet was without sin."[40] "God said to him, ... 'You are a priest forever, in the order of Melchizedek.'"[41]

What is the work of a High Priest? He does many things. He is a wise Counsellor. Isaiah says, "His name shall be called Wonderful, Counsellor."[42] He is a Friend of sinners.[43] He is the Physician who heals our diseases.[44] He is a divine Psychiatrist who restores in us our "right mind."[45] He is an Advocate when Iblis accuses us.[46] He is an Intercessor in the judgment, and an Intercessor even now when we are accused, for "he is able to save completely those who come to God through him, because he always lives to intercede for them. Such a high priest meets our need."[47]

He is also a brother, a term of joy to all who know what it is to have a faithful loving brother in time of need.[48]

All this is what the great High Priest can mean to you, if you will not resist his love. "He always lives," and he is on duty 24 hours a day, seven days a week, 52 weeks a year. His work is that of preparing a people to be ready for his return.

8. *His return is the hope of the world.* He said, "I go to prepare a place for you. And if I go and prepare a place for you, I will come again, and receive you unto myself; that where I am,

---

40. Hebrews 4:14, 15, NIV.
41. Hebrews 5:5, 6, NIV.
42. Isaiah 9:6.
43. Matthew 11:19.
44. Psalm 103:3.
45. Mark 5:15.
46. 1 John 2:1.
47. Hebrews 7:24-26.
48. Hebrews 2:11; Matthew 28:10.

there ye may be also.'"[49] Two angels promised his sorrowing disciples the same: "Why do you stand here looking into the sky? This same Jesus, who has been taken from you into heaven, will come back in the same way you have seen him go into heaven."[50]

The Revelation says: "Look, he is coming with the clouds, and every eye will see him, even those who pierced him; and all the peoples of the earth will mourn because of him. So shall it be! Amen."[51]

The Hadith of Al-Bukhari adds: "Says Muhammed, 'In the name of God who preserves my soul, verily Jesus, the son of Mary, will come soon as the righteous judge.'"[52] Says the Qur'an: "What do they look for but that God shall come to them in the shadows of the clouds with the angel [or, with angels, tr. by Maulana Muhammed Ali]? Then the case would be already judged. All cases are returned to God."[53]

9. *Lastly, the invitations and demands of Jesus are unique.* Everyone can know for himself the truth of his promise: "Come to me, all you who are weary and burdened, and I will give you rest. ... You will find rest for your souls. For my yoke is easy and my burden is light."[54] He demands absolutely everything from us, and he has the right to demand this because he has already given everything in sacrifice for us:

> If anyone would come after me, he must deny himself and take up his cross and follow me. For whoever wants to save his life will lose it, but whoever loses his life for me will find it. ... For the Son of Man is going to come in his Father's

---

49. John 14:2, 3.
50. Acts 1:9-11, NIV.
51. Revelation 1:7, NIV.
52. *The Hadith of Al-Bukhari*, vol. 4, p. 205.
53. *The Qur'an*, 2:20.
54. Matthew 11:29, 30.

glory with his angels, and then he will reward each person according to what he has done.[55]

Is Jesus a real historical character, or just a myth invented by some dreamy visionaries?

The Gospel records of his life are documents that abound in precise historical, geographical, linguistic, and cultural corroborations. Documentary fragments survive from within a few years of the death of one of Jesus' apostles, providing very early confirmation of the Gospel accounts.

Truth is stranger than fiction. No one, past or present, could have invented a character, in whom there was such profound disclosure of the love of God. A love even willing to go to a cross to die! The love revealed in the records of the Gospels is unworldly, beyond man's imagination. Its only source must be supernatural Satanic, or heavenly. It is impossible that Satan could have invented such a pure, selfless love as we see in Jesus. Therefore its source can only be heavenly.

The Jewish priests, the Pharisees, and the doctors of their law, were foremost in rejecting Jesus as their Messiah. Yet the prophecies of the Old Testament Scriptures find precise fulfilment in him. (See Appendix A, p. 205.)

The prophetic searchlight of the ages focuses on Jesus as the long-awaited Messiah, typified in countless blood sacrifices for thousands of years, and foretold in the predictions of the prophets.

When subjected to the closest legal and historical scrutiny, the Gospel accounts of the resurrection of Jesus, and of the disciples' behaviour, demonstrate that his death and resurrection were valid historical events. (See Appendix B, p. 211.) It is impossible that eleven disciples of Jesus, plus hundreds of witnesses, could form a conspiracy to convince the world of a mythical resurrection, and not one when tortured would confess that they had lied.

---

55. Matthew 16:24-27, NIV

The notorious Watergate conspiracy in the 1970's concerned about ten men sworn to be loyal to a central figure. Yet the mere fear of embarrassment or imprisonment impelled all of them to tell the truth in order to save themselves. If the resurrection of Jesus from the dead were not true, surely those eleven apostles would have broken down and confessed that the whole story was a fabrication. Nothing but the truth could have caused those apostles and Paul to maintain to their dying whispers, that Jesus indeed rose from the dead.

If we saw a huge tree flourishing in a desert waste, we would know that it was not only planted there, but that an underground stream of water continually nourishes its buried roots. The teachings of Jesus, accepted by millions of early believers, turned the Roman world upside down. Persecuted, proscribed, martyred, the early followers of Jesus bravely died for their faith in him. Yet, if he was merely a mythical character, who could have gathered the strength to endure fiendish persecution for his sake, to say nothing of torture and death?

And what could account for the millions of lives transformed today by the teachings of Jesus? As the Holy Bible has penetrated to far distant primitive peoples, their villages have been changed from the darkness of heathenism to the light of the love of Jesus. Alcoholics, drug abusers, prostitutes, criminals, have been converted. There is a living stream that nourishes those roots!

Can the example and teachings of Jesus be considered valuable and practical for the everyday life of mankind in general? He never married; can he be an example to mankind who do marry and have families? He refused to defend himself or his disciples with the sword; is this practical? He said that we should "not resist an evil person. If someone strikes you on the right cheek, turn to him the other also." [56] Is this common sense?

---

56. Matthew 5:39, NIV

As One sent of God, more than a mere prophet, Jesus knows how to counsel husbands and wives. During his earthly life he truly "was in all points tempted like as we are, yet without sin."[56] He is "Immanuel, ... God with us."[57] His teachings produce happy marriages.

He taught that ultimate power does not rest with the sword, "for all they that take the sword shall perish with the sword."[58] Ultimate power rests in love! Is this practical, beneficial truth? History repeatedly demonstrates the futility of wars as a method of solving problems. God has spoken to mankind in the words of Jesus; and only woe has come to peoples or nations who reject his teaching.

Jesus' command not to "resist an evil person" makes sense in its true context. Here he demonstrates his right to the sublime title, "Prince of peace." How many millions, yes billions, of poor people's dollars (or pounds) are wasted in vain lawsuits, attacks, counter-attacks, and endless quarrels! The simple "Golden Rule" taught by Jesus would solve almost all of these problems, for it says: "All things whatsoever ye would that men should do to you, do ye even so to them: for this is the law and the prophets."[59]

In this light it can be seen that Jesus is the world's rightful Ruler, for he taught pure, common sense, practical righteousness. The unbelieving world has never given his teaching a fair trial, and we shall have to wait for its ultimate practical demonstration in the "new heavens and new earth, wherein dwelleth righteousness."[60] In the meantime, the believer who follows him will have peace even in a topsy-turvy world, for the divine principle of love "never fails."[61]

---

56. Hebrews 4:15.
57. Matthew 1:23.
58. Matthew 26:52.
59. Matthew 7:12.
60. 2 Peter 3:13.
61. 1 Corinthians 13:8.

He calls you today, as he called his first disciples, to give all for him. Matthew, when he heard the invitation, "left all, rose up, and followed him."[62] And don't forget that Matthew was a wealthy businessman! Peter, Andrew, John, and others were fishermen, and left a phenomenal haul of fish untouched, to follow him.[63]

What authority he has! And people the world round respond the same way.

Why?

The answer: his love, his authority, his power to save, his divine power over the hearts of all men. He humbled himself, making himself of no reputation. And remember: he will refuse absolutely no one who comes to him, for he has promised: "Him that cometh to me I will in no wise cast out."[64] That includes you.

---

62. Luke 5:28.
63. Luke 5:3-11.
64. John 6:37.

I acknowledge my indebtedness to Dr. Charles Marsh for the outline of this chapter.

"For their saying, 'We slew the Messiah, Jesus, son Mary, the messenger of Allah.' Yet they did not slay him neither crucified him. It only appeared so unto them."
(*The Qur'an*, 4:157).

12

The Man Who Bore the Mysterious Curse of God, and Yet Lived

Never before had the world seen such a strange happening, neither has it seen anything like it since: a *good* man was hanged on a cross where he bore the curse of God. And yet he lived!

It was never Allah's intention that the cross should become the emblem of idolatry that so many people make of it. Those who make an idol of the cross and bow down to it, or hang it on their walls, or set it up on steeples, or wear it around their necks, misunderstand the meaning of the cross. Allah never intended that wars should be fought under the symbol of the cross, or that it should become an emblem of imperialism or injustice. Satan has become a very clever enemy, and has perverted a necessary truth about Allah in order to blind people.

What does the cross mean?

Long ago, the great Musa declared to all mankind that anyone who is hanged on a tree (or a cross) is under the curse of God; and everybody believed it:

> If a man guilty of a capital offence is put to death and his body is hung on a tree, you must not leave his body on the

tree overnight. Be sure to bury him that same day, because anyone who is hung on a tree is under God's curse. [1]

Everybody knows how bitterly the Jews hated Jesus. He declared that he was the manifestation of I AM who had led Israel out of Egyptian bondage; he declared also that he had existed before the time of our "father" Abraham. This made the Jews so angry that they took up stones to kill him.[2] They sent spies hoping to catch him making some little mistake that they could use as an excuse to condemn him. No man has ever been hated as was Jesus. In fact, the nature of the opposition he had to meet was itself a miracle, and says something important to us. It was human sin blossoming out after thousands of years into its full fruit—"enmity against God."

This ultimate opposition came when the high priest of Israel angrily confronted him with a direct question: "In the name of the living God I now put you on oath: tell us if you are the Messiah, the Son of God."

Jesus answered straightforwardly, yes. This does not mean that he claimed that God had slept with a woman and produced him in that manner, for that would be a blasphemous thing. But it meant that he claimed to be born of a virgin, the only man in all history born in this way, and that he stood in an intimate relationship to God, a relationship unique for all time. (In everyday speech we use the term "son of" in a metaphorical sense. In Arabic, *ibn al haram* means a bad man; we speak of "sons of thunder." The term "son" here means *like*.)

The Jews were so angry that they decided on the spot, "'He is guilty and must die.' Then they spat in his face and beat him; and those who slapped him said, 'Prophesy for us, Messiah! Guess who hit you!'" [3]

---

1. Deuteronomy 21:22, 23, NIV.
2. John 8:57-59.
3. Matthew 26:63-68, TEV.

Why This Hatred?

The world today shudders with horror at cruel things that terrorists do to innocent people. But the hatred and cruelty shown to Jesus is the strangest the world has ever seen, because it was directed against a man who was utterly good and loving, a man who worked miracles of healing, who spoke only words of divine wisdom, and who gave every evidence of divine appointment and divine character. Why this mysterious hatred against Allah's "Word"?

> And the angel said, "O Mary, Lo! Allah giveth thee glad tidings of a Word from him whose name is the Messiah, Jesus, son of Mary, illustrious in the world and the hereafter and one of those brought near unto Allah." [4]

The secret of the priests' enmity comes out in the open in the story of their second attempt to stone him. He had said, "'I and the Father are one.'" They were so enraged that they lost their sense of self-control and balanced judgment. They picked up stones to kill him.

Calmly and courageously he faced the crowd and asked simply, "'I have shown you many great miracles from the Father. For which of these do you stone me?'"

This question caught them off guard for a moment. Then they replied: "'We are not stoning you for any of these, ... but for blasphemy, because you, a mere man, claim to be God.'" [5]

Could he have been right when he made that claim?

One thing is sure and certain: the hatred shown by his enemies was not inspired by Allah! It could have only one other source: Iblis himself.

And why did Satan hate him so? Why does he hate him who is Allah's "Word"? Satan's age-long hatred of Allah was coming out in the open at last.

---

4. *The Qur'an*, 3:44.
5. John 10:30-33, NIV.

Could it be that Allah was indeed revealing himself in a form that humans could understand? Could Satan see something the Jewish priests could not see? Did he recognize in Jesus the author of faith, the One who had appeared to Abraham, the One typified by the "tremendous Victim" offered to "ransom" Abraham's son and all his descendants?

His character shines brightest under the abuse he suffered at the hands of wicked, sneering, murderous people. When accused and maligned and lied about, he meekly remained silent. Any other good man, under such pressure, would call down Heaven's curses on his tormentors. When one of his own disciples faltered in human weakness and denied him, we read, Jesus only looked at him sadly, the disappointment showing in his face, but he expressed no reproach. Even when another of his disciples, a traitor, betrayed him with a hypocritical kiss, he did not get angry, but said, "'Friend, why have you come?'" [6] While the two thieves crucified with him were screaming and shouting obscenities at the soldiers, Jesus prayed for his murderers: "Father, forgive them, for they know not what they do." [7]

These are not the credentials of any ordinary man. No other human being had ever shown such divine love. As he hung on the cross, stripped naked and despised by the people, he never lost his patience. Something dreadfully mysterious was happening. No other man in all history had suffered like this!

Two astounding things had met in a head-on collision: (a) The mysterious hatred of Satan for God, a hatred manifested in the murderous actions of Jesus' enemies; and (b) the marvelous love of Allah grappling with that hatred hand to hand at the cross. It was a battle between Allah and Satan. The whole world was represented in the guilt of the unjust condemnation of Jesus: the Jews, who instigated it; the

---

6. Matthew 26:50, NIV, margin.
7. Luke 23:34.

European Romans, who in cowardice would go along with the crime; and the great crowds of onlookers who would do nothing to save an innocent man. Even his own disciples, who had the best opportunity of anyone to know who he was, turned tail and ran for their lives, leaving him to suffer alone. Not one soul came forward to defend him in his hour of need! No one even offered him a drink of water in his agony.

The only one to give him any help was Simon of Cyrene, an African who carried his heavy cross for him when he fainted beneath its weight. And even he was forced to do so by the Roman soldiers.

The tree to which Jesus was nailed was only a wooden cross; the real cross, which is timeless, was the collision of Satan's will against God's will, which took place on that same Mt. Moriah where Abraham had once been called to offer up his beloved son.

The Holy Injil reveals the truth: that hatred was an outburst of "enmity against God,"[8] like a slumbering volcano bursting for the in sudden eruption. Long before the red-hot lava and sulphurous flames shoot upwards from the fiery mountain, the fires are smouldering underneath. So "enmity against God" has been the subterranean hatred which has smouldered in human hearts since sin began. It has produced endless wars and quarrels. Allah permitted it to be unmasked at the cross so all could see it clearly.

This passionate human rage was vented on Jesus. His enemies discerned beneath his meek and lowly exterior the inward evidence that he was akin to Allah, and this was why they hated him so. Of course, they didn't realize it, but they were nonetheless guilty. This tells us something significant about the nature and character of the man they crucified! Supernatural hatred required a supernatural victim!

---

8. Romans 8:7.

The Deep Meaning of the Cross

Ever since the prophet Musa had declared that anyone who is hanged on a tree is "under God's curse," death on the cross was regarded as something worse than death itself. If a judge sentenced a criminal to die by having a sword thrust through his heart, he could still have something to be happy about: he could pray to Allah and beg forgiveness and die with the assurance of a place in Paradise. Even if the judge sentenced him to die by stoning, he could still believe that Allah would hear his dying prayer.

But if the judge said, "I sentence you to die on a tree," the poor wretch was doomed according to popular belief. Allah will never hear him pray, for he is "under God's curse." This is how the world understood the prophet Musa's words. Such a condemned person was forever accursed, and therefore a human write-off, lost.

It doesn't help to say that this was fair. The great Musa said it, and everybody believed it. There was a reason for it. (Actually, only the vilest of hardened criminals were ever executed this way.) It was an anticipation of the cross of Jesus.

So bitter was the Jews' hatred of Jesus, that when the Roman governor Pilate asked them what they wanted done with him, they cried out, "'Crucify him!'"

"'Why? What crime has he committed?'

"But they shouted all the louder, 'Crucify him!'"

The pagan Roman governor had more sense of justice than had the Jews. "'I am innocent of this man's blood,' he said, 'It is your responsibility!'

"All the people answered, 'Let his blood be on us and on our children!'" [9] Those words were written by an eyewitness, John, nearly 2,000 years ago. He heard the very words. And

---

9. Matthew 27:22-25, NIV.

the words of ancient manuscripts of the Holy Injil are among the most accurately preserved of any in the world.

It is difficult not to recognize that the answer of the Jews has indeed been fulfilled in the terrible destruction of Jerusalem in A.D. 70, the dissolution of their nation, and their almost unbelievable sufferings ever since. To recognize this fact is not anti-Semitism. It has always been wrong to try to punish innocent people for wrongs their ancestors did. And the Jewish leaders who hated Jesus were no worse than all other sinful humans. In fact, the Holy Injil teaches that all share the guilt.

Was it actually the Son of God whom they rejected? Not one person was ever able to bring against him a charge of sin of any kind. Only this: he claimed to be the Son of God. This alone was their complaint against him.

If they had thought him to be a mere lunatic, they would have recommended imprisonment or banishment. If they had thought him to be an ordinary criminal, they would have recommended death by the sword of stoning. But death by the cross? Why were they so anxious to put a man who claimed to be the Son of God under the "curse" of God?

And did he actually bear the curse of God?

According to Holy Scripture, there are two kinds of death: the ordinary thing which all mortal men suffer; and a second kind, the strange thing known as "the second death."[10] The first death is not the truly terrible one, for Scripture and the Qur'an call it a "sleep," from which there is an awakening at the resurrection. Countless people have died this "sleep," and there is hope and comfort that humans know and feel in such a death.

---

10. Revelation 2:11; 20:14.

The Mysterious "Second Death"

But the "second death" is the real thing, the death of hopelessness and utter despair from which there is to be no resurrection. This will be the fate of all who are eventually lost. It is the sentence of complete, unrelieved condemnation. It is the inward feeling that burns like fire in every cell of one's being, the sense of the hiding of Allah's face, that one is ostracized from his great universe, and from him, utterly friendless, alone cast into outer darkness for ever and ever. The burden of lonely guilt weighs down the soul of the condemned person with an indescribable pain and sorrow.

This is how Allah permitted Jesus to feel on the cross. This is why he cried out, "My God, my God, why hast thou forsaken me?"[11] This was the ultimate step that divine love took in coming down lower and still lower, toward "the death of the cross," the most awful that Satan and his fiends could invent.

This kind of love comes from the heart of Allah alone. It is the divine evidence that Allah sent Jesus as his representative, to pay the penalty of the broken law of Allah, and to redeem the world.

Only by permitting Jesus to endure this experience was it possible for Allah to untie that knot of sinful self-love, pride, and hatred that Satan had tied on mankind when he rebelled against Allah's great government. The human race became alienated from Allah, captives to sin and evil. Jesus endured the curse "of the cross," the most astonishing thing that had ever happened on earth; it has attracted the attention and wonder of the whole world. It can never be hidden or suppressed.

Best of all, it has changed human beings, transforming them from selfish, proud, godless people into humble, pure, loving, true believers who are surrendered to Allah. To have faith in Jesus means to appreciate what he did, and who he was

---

11. Matthew 27:46.

when he did it; and it is to feel a heart appreciation that he took upon himself the world's "enmity against God." Thus he conquered it for ever. He stood in for Allah, taking his place as his representative, taking the blow that was meant for God. This was the greatest thing that ever happened, the "day" that Abraham "saw" by faith and rejoiced in.

Jesus' sacrifice of himself on the cross builds a bridge between alienated man and God, so that the alienation that has stretched like a yawning gulf of darkness between Allah and man is bridged for ever. This made an 'atonement, " or at-one-ment. This how he was that "tremendous Victim" that Allah provided for Abraham's son; and Abraham knew it. He was not so naïve as to imagine that a ram's blood could "ransom" his precious son! Jesus was that "Lamb slain from the foundation of the world,"[12] the true Victim who made the infinite sacrifice of himself on Mt. Moriah.

This was Abraham's faith, for he saw Jesus' day and "was glad."[13] It is the faith of every spiritual child of Abraham, who sees himself as Abraham's beloved, doomed to die on the altar on Mt. Moriah—Abraham's son symbolizes every one of us. We are all alike ransomed by a divine sacrifice!

Why It Was Necessary for Jesus to Die

Scripture does not represent Jesus as a weakling captured by a mob and executed by them. All the soldiers in the world could not have tied his hands if he had not willingly submitted; all the nails in the world could not have held him to a tree if he had chosen to "come down from the cross." No Roman spear could have pierced his body if he had not permitted it.

Did Jesus actually suffer and die on the cross, or did it only *seem* so? Did Allah rescue him and permit someone else to take his place there? These are important questions.

---

12. Revelation 13:8.
13. John 8:56.

If Allah rescued him, there was no "tremendous Victim" to "ransom" Abraham's son, for a mere man's blood can never be an adequate ransom for such a descendant of Abraham.

And if Allah rescued Jesus form the hatred of his enemies, he would also be guilty of contradicting his own true character of love that is willing to step down to the lowest level in order to "ransom" Abraham's descendants. Any love that merely *pretends* to go all the way, but deceptively stops short of the complete sacrifice, becomes a lie, a trick. Allah can never be guilty of such a thing.

And Jesus would never dare to claim a lie, for after his death he said to doubting Thomas, "Reach hither thy finger, and behold my hands; and reach hither thy hand, and thrust it into my side: and be not faithless, but believing."[14] The gaping wound caused by the Roman soldier's spear in his heart would have caused instant death if he had not already been dead. Jesus claimed to be resurrected from the dead.

Further, if Allah rescued his representative, the Word, that would mean that he played himself into the hands of the murderous Jewish priests and the Roman soldiers. The reason is this: they taunted Jesus, saying: "'If you are the king of the Jews, save yourself.'" And the unbelieving thief who was also crucified railed at him: "'Aren't you the Christ? Save yourself and us!'" And the people laughed at him, saying: "'He saved others, ... but he can't save himself! Let this Christ, this King of Israel, come down now from the cross, that we may see and believe.'"[15] These were the taunts of *un*believers who completely misunderstood what was happening. Allah would not demean himself to bargain with people like that. To yield to their taunts and accept their challenge would mean yielding to them the victory of unbelief.

---

14. John 20:27.
15. Luke 23:37, 39; Mark 15:31, 32, NIV.

While it is true that Allah "ransomed" Abraham's son, no substitute was provided for the ram offered in his place. That ram truly died; and "the tremendous Victim" whom the ram symbolized also truly died. Otherwise there could have been no genuine ransom. It would have been a make-believe, a magic trick.

Speaking of the Messiah, the holy prophet Isaiah says: "He hath poured out his soul unto death."[16] The book of Hebrews in the Holy Injil says that "in the days of his flesh" Jesus "offered up prayers and supplications with strong crying and tears unto him that was able to save him from death."[17] But this does not mean that Allah did not let him die, for we read also in Hebrews that Allah "brought again from the dead our Lord Jesus."[18] Allah saved him by permitting him to die as a "tremendous Victim" and then raising him up from death.

If divine love will manoeuvre deceptively in order to save itself, then it is the same as our natural human love, and it ceases to be divine and can no longer be genuine heavenly love. In that case, God's character would be no different from our own, and to worship him would be the same as worshipping ourselves. And that would be gross idolatry all over again—the very thing that Abraham protested against.

Those who crucified Jesus spoke more truth than they realized: Jesus *could not* save himself, because he *would* not. His love would not let him do so. This was in fact the greatest proof that he was the true Messiah, the true "Victim" symbolized by all the blood sacrifices that believers had offered for thousands of years. And in saying such things, the Jews unwittingly condemned themselves as they stood before that cross, for in rejecting Christ as a sacrifice, they rejected what Abraham and all the prophets had believed in for thousands of years.

---

16. Isaiah 53:12.
17. Hebrews 5:7.
18. Hebrews 13:20.

The honoured Qur'an says of the Jews: "For their saying, 'We slew the Messiah, Jesus, son of Mary, the messenger of Allah.' Yet they did not slay him, neither crucified him. It only appeared so to them."[19] These words do not contradict the Injil. Rightly understood, they are a proof that what the eyewitness apostles of Jesus reported is true. These words do not say that Jesus did not die; they say that it was not the Jews or the Romans who actually killed him.

Jesus said: "'I lay down my life—only to take it up again. No one takes it from me, but I lay it down of my own accord. I have authority [power, ability] to lay it down and authority [power, ability] to take it up again. This command I received from my Father.'"[20]

He said the same to the Roman governor, Pilate, who said to him: "'Don't you realize I have power either to free you or to crucify you'"

"Jesus answered, 'You would have no power over me if it were not given to you from above.'"[21]

The honoured Qur'an states that Jesus did actually die: "When Allah said, 'Jesus, I will cause you to die and cause you to ascend to Me, and will cleanse you of those who disbelieve and will set your followers above those who disbelieve until the resurrection day.'"[22] The crucifixion was not the "power" of men—they only imagined so. It was their *will*, yes; but they had no authority unless Allah had permitted it.

In another passage the Qur'an quotes Jesus as predicting his death: "'Peace be upon me, the day I was born, and the day I die, and the day I am raised up alive.' That is Jesus, son of Mary, the word of truth concerning which they are

---

19. *The Qur'an*, 4:157.
20. John 10:17, 18, NIV.
21. John 19:10, 11, NIV.
22. *The Qur'an*, 3:54

doubting."[23] Thus it is clear that the passage, "They slew him not nor crucified, but it only seemed to them so," does not intend to question that Jesus died on the cross. "And they [the Jews] planned and Allah planned, and Allah is the best of planners. When Allah said, 'Jesus, I will take you to Me and will raise you to Me.'"[24] Allah planned it all, for the salvation of mankind! Will you accept his plan?

---

23. *The Qur'an*, 19:33, 34
24. *The Qur'an*, 3:54.

"Upon the day when heaven with the clouds will be split asunder, and the angels will be sent down in majesty. The sovereignty on that day will be the true sovereignty belonging to the all-merciful and it will be a hard day for unbelievers."

(*The Qur'an*, 25:25, 26)

13

The Return of Jesus and the End of the World

It is the love and compassion of Allah that make the return of Jesus necessary. As time goes on, foolish, sinful man is transforming his once beautiful world into a man-made hell. Allah's kindness will not permit this to become complete.

He will therefore intervene by sending Jesus, as he has long foretold by the ancient prophets of the Holy Scriptures. Malachi says that he

> ... shall suddenly come to his temple, even the messenger of the covenant. ... But who may abide the day of his coming? and who shall stand when he appeareth? ... He shall sit as a refiner and purifier of silver.[1]

God's promise of rescue by Jesus is not new. It was cherished from the beginning:

> Enoch also, the seventh from Adam, prophesied of these, saying, Behold, the Lord cometh with ten thousands of his saints, to execute judgment upon all.[2]

---

1. Malachi 3:1-3.
2. Jude 14, 15.

The idea of final judgment to come at the end of the world has been emphasized throughout the Scriptures. The inspired writer of the Psalms (Zabur) describes the glory of that day in these words:

> Our God shall come, and shall not keep silence: a fire shall devour before him, and it shall be very tempestuous round about him. He shall call to the heavens from above, and to the earth, that he may judge his people. [3]

The honoured Qur'an says:

> What do they look for but that Allah shall come to them in the shadows of the clouds with the angels? Then the case will be already judged. All cases are returned to Allah. [4]

> And those who disbelieve will not cease to be in doubt of it until the hour come upon them unawares, or there come unto them the doom of a disastrous day. [5]

But the return of Jesus is a day of gladness for all who truly believe the word of Allah. He comes to rescue them from oppression under Iblis. The prophet Isaiah tells us that the resurrection from the dead will take place at his coming:

> He will swallow up death in victory; and the Lord God will wipe away tears from off all faces; and the rebuke of his people shall he take away from off all the earth: for the Lord hath spoken it. And it shall be said in that day ... We have waited for him, and he will save us: this is the Lord; we have waited for him, we will be glad and rejoice in his salvation. [6]

The book of Al-Bukhari encourages us to look for the return of Jesus: "Says Muhammad, 'In the name of God who preserves my soul, verily Jesus, the son of Mary, will come

---

3. Psalm 50:3, 4.
4. *The Qur'an*, 2:210.
5. The Qur'an 22:55.
6. Isaiah 25:8, 9.

soon as the righteous judge.'" [7] If we trust in our own merits and good deeds in order to justify ourselves in that day of Judgment, we may well tremble in fear. No man or woman can do enough good deeds to drown out the whisperings of the deepest convictions from within the human soul that remind us that all our own righteousness is in vain. But if we have learned the lesson of righteousness by faith, from Abraham, and by faith we are his true descendants, then the Day of Judgment will hold no terrors for us. Says the honoured Qur'an:

> We set up a just balance for the day of resurrection, so that not one soul shall be wronged anything. Even if it be the weight of one grain of mustard seed. We shall produce it, and We are sufficient for reckoners; and We gave Moses and Aaron the criterion, and a light and a reminder for the God-fearing. Those who fear God in secret and who dread the hour. This is a blessed reminder that we have revealed. Will you then reject it? [8]

No, by Allah's grace, we shall not reject it! We shall put our trust in that "tremendous Victim" who has ransomed our souls. Such trust is a million times more effective than trusting to our own merits and good deeds which is in reality the old idolatry that Abraham our father taught us to be done with! We cannot worship Allah alone and also trust our own works of merit!

Why the Return of Jesus?

We can more easily understand the reason if we think of a father's love for his helpless child who is kidnapped and tortured by wicked people. A father may be ever so kind and gentle as a neighbour and friend; but if his little child is being abused, you will see him become angry. History is the

---

7. *The Book of Al-Bukhari*, vol. 4, p. 205.
8. The Qur'an, 21:47-50.

story of the great controversy between Allah and Iblis. Satan's hatred was manifested in the rejection of Jesus; but the book of Revelation declares that the anger of Iblis is now directed against "the inhabiters of the earth" "for the devil is come down unto you, having great wrath, because he knoweth that he hath but a short time." [9] His special anger is against Allah's true believers, "who keep the commandments of God, and have the testimony of Jesus Christ."[10]

In fact, the crowning act of Satan's murderous hatred will be a universal death decree issued against God's people. Revelation describes the final issues of this great controversy. The symbols of the "beast" and its "image" represent man's final rebellion against Allah:

> He ... causeth the earth and them which dwell therein to worship the first beast, whose deadly wound was healed. And he doeth great wonders, so that he maketh fire come down from heaven on the earth in the sight of men ... saying to them that dwell on the earth, that they should make an image to the beast ... and cause that as many as would not worship the image of the beast should be killed.[11]

Here is the reason for the return of Christ! He comes on a rescue mission in behalf of those who choose to be loyal to Allah in the face of this final persecution.

The world is even now moving steadily toward that final climax. As Allah's message of truth penetrates the entire world, human beings will choose their final allegiance, either to receive Allah's "seal," or Satan's clever but bold counterfeit, "the mark of the beast."

Every human being will make his final choice when the principles of both loyalty and rebellion are made clear to his understanding. Allah's compassion will see to it that "the

---

9. Revelation 12:12.
10. Revelation 12:17
11. Revelation 13:12-15.

earth" is to be "lightened" with the "glory" of his last-day message of glad tidings, for a "voice from heaven" will call his true believers to "come out" of "Babylon," "that ye be not partakers of her sins, and that ye receive not of her plagues. For her sins have reached unto heaven, and God hath remembered her iniquities."[12] The Injil says that when "this gospel [good news] of the kingdom shall be preached in all the world for a witness unto all nations," "then shall the end come." [13]

Allah's people will not be afraid in that dreadful day. An inspired prophet spoke beautiful, eloquent words:

> The Name of the Lord comes from afar,
>   with burning anger and dense clouds of smoke:
> His lips are full of wrath,
>   and His tongue is a consuming fire. ...
> He shakes the nations in the sieve of destruction. ...
>
> And you will sing
>   as on the night you celebrate a holy festival;
> your hearts will rejoice
>   as when people go up with flutes
> to the mountain of the Lord.[14]

Praise be to Allah for his faithfulness to those who revere him! "He that dwelleth in the secret place of the most High shall abide under the shadow of the Almighty. ... He shall cover thee with his feathers, and under his wings shalt thou trust: his truth shall be thy shield and buckler. ... Because thou hast made ... the most High, thy habitation; there shall no evil befall thee, neither shall any plague come nigh thy dwelling. For he shall give his angels charge over thee, to keep thee in all thy ways."[15]

---

12. Revelation 18:1-5
13. Matthew 24:14.
14. Isaiah 30:27-29, NIV.
15. Psalm 91:1-11.

How Abraham's Hopes Will Finally Be Realized

The honoured Qur'an reminds us to look forward to that greatest day of all human history:

> And remind them of the day when the trumpet will be blown, and all who are in the heavens and the earth will start in fear saver him whom Allah willeth. And all come to him humbled.[16]
>
> And remember when Allah said, O Jesus, Lo I am gathering thee and causing thee to ascend unto Me and am cleansing thee of those who disbelieve until the day of resurrection. Then unto Me ye will all return, and I shall judge between you as to that wherein ye used to differ.[17]

The Scriptures give us many more details, to describe the return of Jesus: "Unto them that look for him shall he appear the second time without sin unto salvation."[18] He will appear to *all*, for "he cometh with clouds; and every eye shall see him, and they also which pierced him: and all kindreds of the earth shall wail because of him."[19] But those who believe Allah's holy Word will find him a welcome guest "unto salvation."

His coming will be personal and literal, for when he ascended to heaven, two angels told his followers, "This same Jesus, which is taken up from you into heaven, shall so come in like manner as ye have seen him go into heaven."[20] Jesus himself promised, "I will come again, and receive you unto myself; that where I am, there ye may be also."[21] His coming is called "the blessed hope,"[22] a hope that produces joy.

---

16. The Qur'an, 27:87.
17. The Qur'an 3:54.
18. Hebrews 9:28.
19. Revelation 1:7.
20. Acts 1:11.
21. John 14:3.
22. Titus 2:13.

He will resurrect those who have died in faith: "The Lord himself shall descend from heaven with a shout, with the voice of the archangel, and with the trump of God: and the dead in Christ shall rise first."[23]

Abraham's true descendants who have chosen to be loyal to Allah in the face of the final onslaught of Satan will be caught up to meet the Lord. "Then we which are alive and remain shall be caught up together with them in the clouds, to meet the Lord in the air: and so shall we ever be with the Lord. Wherefore comfort one another with these words."[24]

Those who have chosen final rebellion against Allah will not be able to endure the glorious sight of the coming of Jesus in judgment: As the lightning cometh out of the east, and shineth even unto the west; so shall also the coming of the Son of man be.[25]

> The heaven departed as a scroll when it is rolled together; and every mountain and island were moved out of their places. And the kings of the earth, and the great men, and the rich men, and the chief captains and the mighty men ... said to the mountains and rocks, Fall on us, and hide us from the face of him that sitteth on the throne, and from the wrath of the Lamb: for the great day of his wrath is come; and who shall be able to stand? [26]

> God is just: He will pay back trouble to those who trouble you and give relief to you who are troubled, and to us as well. This will happen when the Lord Jesus is revealed from heaven in blazing fire with his powerful angels. He will punish those who do not know God and do not obey the gospel of our Lord Jesus.[27]

---

23. 1 Thessalonians 4:16.
24. 1 Thessalonians 4:17, 18.
25. Matthew 24:27.
26. Revelation 6:14-17.
27. 2 Thessalonians 1:6-8, NIV.

The book of Revelation reveals a grand secret: God has separated the resurrection of the righteous from that of the wicked by 1,000 years, during which time Iblis is to be "bound" so that he can deceive the nations no more until those 1,000 years are ended.[28] Since the Scriptures make plain that the resurrected righteous and the living believers will be caught up with Jesus at his return,[29] this means that the wicked will be slain by the brightness of his return,[30] and will await their resurrection to take place at the end of the 1,000 years.[31] Satan can do nothing to annoy the saints of Allah who are taken away, and of course he can do nothing to the wicked unbelievers who are slain. Thus he is "bound" during this period. The final judgment will be stupendous in scope, beyond our imagination!

The justice and compassion of Allah are seen again in the grand events to take place at the close of the thousand years. The wicked are resurrected to face their judgment, and Iblis resumes with them his evil work of deception, being "loosed out of his prison." He goes forth "to deceive the nations, ... to gather them together to battle: the number of whom is as the sand of the sea." He persuades them one last time to join him in an orgy of rebellion against Allah, motivated by murderous intent. Allah's final judgment is made manifest to the legions of men and angels who watch the spectacle. The wicked have pronounced their own final, tragic judgment; they have demonstrated fully that they have made their ultimate choice to join in high treason against Allah's righteous government of love and justice. Since to prolong their lives in rebellion would only be to prolong their abject misery, Allah mercifully permits "fire ... [to come down] out of heaven" to "devour

---

28. Revelation 20:1-7.
29. 1 Thessalonians 4:16, 17.
30. 2 Thessalonians 2:8.
31. Revelation 20:7, 12, 13.

them." "And death and hell were cast into the lake of fire. This is the second death."[32]

Rebels who will not surrender to justice must be punished with "the second death." Otherwise, the peace and security of Allah's great universe will be in danger. Sin and its offspring, death, must come to a final end. No eternally burning hell full of condemned people's blasphemies will pollute a happy Paradise. "The wicked shall not be: yea, thou shalt diligently consider his place, and it shall not be."[33] "The day that cometh shall burn them up, saith the Lord of hosts, that it shall leave them neither root nor branch."[34] The "eternal fire" is eternal in its consequences—there will be no resurrection following this "second death." It is a libel on the character of a holy and just Allah to picture him as roasting and torturing the lost for endless ages as though he were some Mafia-like monster of sadistic cruelty. The Holy Book does not teach such a slanderous view of Allah's character.

For long ages, Allah has comforted his faithful people with the promise that he will "create new heavens and a new earth: and the former [with its tears and sorrows] shall not be remembered, nor come into mind."[35] After the destruction of Iblis and his evil angels and the wicked who have joined them, Allah will cleanse this cursed old earth with fire, and then create a "new heaven and a new earth."[36]

The day of the Lord will come as a thief in the night; in the which the heavens shall pass away with a great noise, and the elements shall melt with fervent heat, the earth also and the works that are therein shall be burned up. ... Nevertheless we,

---

32. Revelation 20:13, 14.
33. Psalm 37:10.
34. Malachi 4:1.
35. Isaiah 65:17
36. Revelation 21:1.

according to his promise, look for new heavens, and a new earth, wherein dwelleth righteousness.[37]

The Glorious New Heavens and New Earth

Pain, sickness, funerals, corruption, bribery cruelty, war, starvation, disappointment, poverty, homelessness—all these evils will be gone forever. No wonder the return of Jesus is called "the blessed hope." Allah has manifested himself as a mighty Saviour. His enemies are no more. He has shown that love is stronger than hatred, and light is stronger than darkness. He has wrestled Iblis down to death and hell itself, and put an end to sin. The redeemed sing his praises to all eternity.

The joy of the redeemed will not be childish, selfish enjoyment of sensual pleasures. Hazrat Abraham was called "the friend of God" as well as "the father of the faithful." And the redeemed will be, like him, friends of Allah. Their joy is not self-centered, for self-centeredness is the essence of sin and idolatry. But they will share with Abraham the final fulfillment of Allah's promise that he should be "the heir of the world," not cursed by sin as it is now, but made as perfect as the "new earth."[38] (See Romans 4:13.)

They have found something to be concerned about that is vastly greater than their own personal security and reward. Like a true bride who is concerned for her husband's honour, they are caught up in the most thrilling motivation that human hearts can ever know—sympathy with Allah is his grand plan of redemption and his victory over Satan. They appreciate his love "that passeth knowledge," love that was revealed in the sacrifice of that "tremendous Victim" who died for our sins upon a cross on Mt. Moriah.

---

37. 2 Peter 3:10-13.
38. Isaiah 65:17.

How Allah Today Manifests His Love to Each Person

Meanwhile, as we wait for that glad day to come, we are not left alone like orphans in this dark world. Allah's continuing love and compassion are infinite, for he himself is infinite; and even though those who believe in him may number many millions, his grace is given to each one in a measure as full as if that individual were the only person on earth.

The means by which Allah thus blesses every believer in him is the Holy Spirit. The Scriptures exalt the love of Allah, the glory and grandeur of his character. One of his names I "Immanuel, God with us"—with us in the sense of his being a Comforter. Speaking through the ancient prophet Isaiah, Allah says:

> Fear thou not; for I am with thee: be not dismayed; for I am thy God: I will strengthen thee; yea, I will help thee; yea, I will uphold thee with the right hand of my righteousness.[39]

How can the infinite, glorious Allah, "the high and lofty One that inhabiteth eternity,"[40] be "with us" and hold our hand? Is he not too great to notice us poor creatures of the dust? He says further: "I dwell in the high and holy place, with him also that is of a contrite and humble spirit." "To this man will I look, even to him that is poor and of a contrite spirit, and trembleth at my word."[41] The great Allah of eternity does indeed condescend to notice the weakest mortal who believes in him!

If you were the only human being on earth, you could not get more sunshine that you get now as one of more than four thousand million people on the globe. A mother may

---

39. Isaiah 41:10.
40. Isaiah 57:15.
41. Isaiah 66:2.

have many children, but she does not divide her love among them; she loves each one with all her love.

The Close Fellowship of the Holy Spirit

Jesus promised the gift of the Holy Spirit to "abide" with all who believe. This is the secret of their endless joy. they are never lonely!

> I will pray the Father, and he shall give you another Comforter, that he may abide with you for ever; even the Spirit of truth; whom the world cannot receive, because it seeth him not, neither knoweth him: but ye know him; for he dwelleth with you, and shall be in you. I will not leave you comfortless: I will come to you.[42]

The word "Comforter" in the original language is *parakletos*, from two words, *para* meaning "alongside of," as two railroad tracks are always parallel; and *kletos*, meaning "called." Documentary evidence dating from the time of the Roman Emperor Hadrian, about A.D. 125, confirms the Gospel of John; and very early translations of John's Gospel demonstrate that he did indeed write the word *parakletos*, which can refer only to the Holy Spirit. No Greek manuscript from the early centuries has a different word.[43] Jesus' context makes it clear that "Comforter" cannot refer to any mortal man.

The enemy of God and man hates the truth of the divine Comforter promised to every sincere believer, for if Iblis can succeed in breaking that connection of "Immanuel, God with us," he can alienate our souls from the close fellowship with Allah that he wants to establish. Jesus declared the Holy Spirit

---

42. John 14:16-18.
43. In non-Biblical Greek, *parakletos* has the general meaning of "intercessor," a "helper." The verb *parakaleo* occurs in the New Testament about 100 times, indicating that Jesus' use of *parakletos* means "comforter" or "intercessor," one who abides with us. (There is no early Greek manuscript of John's Gospel that has the *periklytos* instead of *parakletos*, and there is no evidence that the word was ever changed by a copyist.)

to be his vicar, his representative; how blasphemous for any mere man to arrogate to himself that position! This was why the book of Revelation attributes to such the word "blasphemy."[44] No mortal man can claim such a divine honour.

The "good news" of the Injil is that through the Holy Spirit, Allah will lead our footsteps to that glorious "new heaven and new earth" that he will create. The prophet Isaiah rightly deserves the honoured title, "the Good News prophet." He explains how near Allah is to all believers:

> The Lord is compassionate, and when you cry to him for help, he will answer you. ... He himself will be there to teach you, and you will not have to search for him any more. If you wander off the road to the right or the left, you will hear his voice behind you saying, "Here is the road. Follow it."[45]

Of course, God is one, so when we read "the Lord" we know it means Allah, "Immanuel, God with us." There is no possibility of our losing the path if we will only listen to his voice, for he stays beside us all the way.

What it all means is that the "good news" of Allah's love and compassion is far better than most people have imagined. The picture is clear: Allah loves us, and he is a Saviour! He is preparing believers to enter Paradise; he is not trying to find some way to keep them out. If we will believe his holy Word, his Holy Spirit will cleanse and sanctify our human hearts.

The reality of the Holy Spirit is a treasure that Allah wants us to appreciate. Says the honoured Qur'an:

> And those messengers, some of whom We have caused to excel others; some there are to whom God spoke, and some of them He exalted in degree, and We gave Jesus, son of Mary, clear proofs, and We confirmed him with the Holy Spirit.[46]

---

44. Revelation 13:6
45. Isaiah 30:19-21, TEV.
46. *The Qur'an*, 2:253.

We indeed created man and We know what his soul whispers within him, and We are nearer to him than his jugular vein.[47]

Allah is the light of the heavens and the earth. The likeness of His light is as a niche wherein is a lamp; the lamp is in a glass; the glass is, as it were, a glittering star kindled from a blessed tree, an olive that is neither of the East nor of the West, whose oil would almost glow forth of itself, though no fire touched it. Light upon light; Allah guides to His light whom He will, and Allah speaks to mankind in allegories, for Allah is Knower of all things.[48]

The Glorious Song of True Believers

As Abraham was a "stranger and a pilgrim" on this earth, so we are pilgrims journeying to Paradise. Allah's "Good News" comforts us every step of the way. Will you not choose to walk in that way?

The holy prophet John saw and heard in heavenly vision the eternal joy that will inspire the most beautiful song ever heard in the new heavens and new earth that Allah will create:

I beheld, and I heard the voice of many angels round about the throne, ... the number of them was ten thousand times ten thousand, and thousands of thousands; saying with a loud voice, Worthy is the Lamb that was slain to receive power, and riches, and wisdom, and strength, and honour, and glory, and blessings. And every creature which is in heaven, and on the earth, and under the earth, and such as are in the sea, and all that are in them, heard I saying, Blessing, and honour, and glory, and power, be unto him that sitteth upon the throne, and unto the Lamb for ever. [49]

Human hearts can *begin* to sing that lovely song even today, for their thrill of gratitude to Allah for his great sacrifice of

---

47. *The Qur'an* 50:16
48. *The Qur'an*, 24:35.
49. Revelation 5:11-13.

love is "the faith of Abraham," the faith of one who is truly surrendered to Allah.

Such faith is true religion. Does your heart respond with that faith? Do you choose to join those "ten thousand times ten thousand, and thousands of thousands" who, like Abraham, say "Amen!"?

"We lifted the mountain of Sinai over them, when We exacted from them their covenant; and said unto them, Enter the gate of the city worshipping. We also said unto them, Transgress not the Sabbath-day. And We received from them a firm covenant, that they would observe these things."

(*The Qur'an*, 4:154)

14
Allah's True Covenant of Sabbath Rest

If someone were to offer you a lorryload of gold, it could not be as valuable as the subject of this chapter: Allah's holy day, his Sabbath.

But it is something that the world as a whole has tried to forget, even though he said, "*Remember* the sabbath day, to keep it holy."[1] History is strewn with many attempts to wipe out the Sabbath rest: the Egyptian bondage of the children of Israel; the Roman Empire's persecution; the French Revolution's attempts to abolish the seven-day week and substitute a ten-day week; modern attempts to change the calendar; and of course, constantly, secularism and materialism.

Still, Allah has written his Sabbath day deep into man's mind the world around. Our universal week of seven days is one memento. Why are there exactly seven days in the week? What natural thing marks off seven days? The word *month* indicates the time marked by the moon's phases; a *year* is the time in which the earth makes its circuit around the sun; a *day* marks

---

1. Exodus 20:11.

the earth's rotation on her axis. Search every encyclopaedia in the world; no scientist or historian can give any clue as to the origin of the week except that God created the heavens and the earth in six days, and rested on the seventh day!

The honoured Qur'an reminds us:

> Your Lord is Allah who created the heavens and the earth in six days, then sat Himself upon the throne. ... Blessed be Allah, the Lord of the worlds.[2]

The seven-day week was observed in Hindustan, by the Brahmins of India, by the ancient Arabs, by the Chinese, by the Greeks and Romans, the Egyptians, even by the Saxons in northern Europe. Hesiod, a pagan Greek poet (circa 900 B.C.) declared that the seventh day is holy, as did Homer and Callimachus, ancient Greek writers.

The origin of the week is stated in the Ten Commandments of Allah:

> Remember the sabbath day, to keep it holy. Six days shalt thou labour and do all thy work; but the seventh day is the sabbath of the Lord thy God. ... For in six days the Lord made heaven and earth, the sea and all that in them is, and rested the seventh day: wherefore the Lord blessed the sabbath day, and hallowed it.[3]

"The fool hath said in his heart, there is no God."[4] Unbelieving scientists have tried to tell us that there was no creation in six days, that the earth and its teeming life just happened through random processes called "evolution" over many millions of years. And people who are unwilling or unable to examine the evidence for themselves have assumed that scientists cannot be wrong.

But there is no solid proof for random evolution which denies the Bible story. It remains only a theory. If evolution

---

2. *The Qur'an*, 7:54.
3. Exodus 20:8-11.
4. Psalm 14:1.

is true, we are all highly developed animals, and the law of the jungle must ultimately become supreme. Wars, crime immorality, are steadily pushing us closer to that jungle! But in recent years there has come a widespread movement of highly educated scientists who question the evolutionary theories, and believe there is no good scientific reason to doubt the Bible record of creation. Their answer to evolution is "Creationism."

The Sabbath is Allah's memorial of that creation, his universal gift to the world. It is no more Jewish than Abraham was Jewish. Thousands of years before there was a Jew, Allah "blessed the seventh day, and sanctified it: because that in it he had rested from all his work."[5] To "bless" and "sanctify" it means to fill it with physical, social, and spiritual enrichment for the life of man, and to set it apart as eternally sacred, the day dedicated to Allah, and filled with happiness for man.

The holy Sabbath has marked off every week that has come and gone since that first one of creation. Noah obviously kept the Sabbath.[6] Allah said of Hazrat Abraham, "I know him, that he ... shall keep the way of the Lord, to do justice and judgment."[7] That includes keeping the Sabbath, for the prophet Isaiah makes it clear that keeping the Sabbath is an essential part of "justice and judgment":

> Keep ye judgment, and do justice ... Blessed is the man that doeth this, and the son of man that layeth hold on it; that keepeth the sabbath from polluting it, and keepeth his hand from doing any evil.[8]

This means that our father Abraham was also a keeper of Allah's holy Sabbath. And the covenant that he made with him

---

5. Genesis 2:1-3
6. Genesis 7:7; 8:10.
7. Genesis 18:19
8. Isaiah 56:1, 2.

included the keeping of the Sabbath, for he says "Abraham ... obeyed my commandments":

> Also the sons of the stranger, that join themselves to the Lord, to serve him, and to love the name of the Lord, to be his servants, every one that keepeth the sabbath from polluting it, and taketh hold of my covenant; even them will I ... make joyful in my house of prayer.[9]

Since Abraham is "the father of all them that believe," the keeping of Allah's holy Sabbath is a part of true faith in him. And he gives the blessing of the Sabbath to non-Jews on the same basis that he gives non-Jews the gifts of sunshine and rain! The Sabbath is a precious gift for the whole world to enjoy. Say the Injil, "The Sabbath was made for *man*."[10] It was made for everyone who inhabits the earth that Allah created in six days! It is a gift, a blessing; no one is to be deprived.

There is a special benefit connected with the Sabbath, for "God blessed the seventh *day*."[11] *People* can be blessed by him on any day of the week, for "he maketh his sun to rise on the evil and on the good, and sendeth rain on the just and on the unjust;"[12] but there is a special benefit on the Sabbath *day*, a blessing which comes only with the Sabbath, the blessing of spiritual rest. It has not been placed on any other day and cannot be found anywhere else. Many do not know about it.

What is there in the Sabbath that is so wonderful?

It gives us a link to the Creator so that our roots are firmly established in his covenant family. This produces within us a divinely imparted sense of self-worth; we did not just "happen." We have been created and redeemed by Allah.

---

9. Isaiah 56:6, 7; see also Genesis 26:5.
10. Mark 2:28.
11. Genesis 2:2
12. Matthew 5:45.

We are not here because of *chance* but because of his direct *choice*. As sons and daughters of Abraham, we are included in the great covenant Allah made with him. Tragedies and sorrows may surround us, but we know that we are involved in his great plan for the redemption of this world.

This is included in the rest provided in the Sabbath day. It gives meaning to life; without it, the confusion and injustice in this world become unbearable to our human soul and conscience. The Sabbath is our insignia of membership in the covenant family of God, the proof that we are a part, though ever so small, of his great plan of redemption: "Keep my sabbaths holy, that they may be a sign between us. Then you will know that I am the Lord you God."[13]

The Sabbath provides true rest for the soul. The word itself means rest. Allah worked six days and rested the seventh. Spiritual rest is delicious; for this reason, it is the Sabbath that imparts meaning to the other six days. The presence of his Spirit is in the day that he has "blessed" and "sanctified."

He promised Moses (Musa), "My presence shall go with thee, and I will give thee rest."[14] Rest comes from enjoying the "presence" of God. He is unseen; and no temple made with hands can contain his holy presence. Hazrat Abraham was right to turn from the worship of all "seen" idols, to worship the one true *un*seen Allah. His true temple is not a thing of stone or of wood or of plaster. This is why his blessing of rest is in his holy Sabbath.

The Sabbath delivers us from the rat-race of self-seeking in a world of materialism. It provides "rest" from the pressure of selfishly trying to get ahead. The constant driving force of aggression, whether in school, business, politics, or

---

13. Ezekiel 20:20, NIV.
14. Genesis 33:14.

social life, wears out our life forces. These are dehumanizing, demoralizing pressures; even modern advertising keeps us in a constant state of wanting something we don't have. This can kill true happiness.

Just as Allah rested on the Sabbath, so he says, "in it thou shalt not do any work."[15] Although this is not an enforced rest, his commandment does deliver us from the slavery of our own inner compulsion to work to make more money. Thus the Sabbath commandment is liberation, providing freedom from ourselves, and from our oppressive environment. In obedience to Allah's loving commandment, we do not work on his holy day. He adds:

> If you keep your feet from breaking the Sabbath
>   and from doing as you please on my holy day,
> if you call the Sabbath a delight
>   and the Lord's holy day honourable,
> and if you honour it by not going your own way
>   and not doing as you please or speaking idle words,
> then you will find your joy in the Lord.[16]

True wealth is spiritual, not materialistic. Both pauper and prince appear in the presence of God on the Sabbath, side by side. A wise writer has said, "The Sabbath teaches us to commune rather than to compete with one another."[17] There would be no wars if nations kept the Sabbath!

Sabbath-keeping reinforces our participation in the faith of Abraham. Allah said of him, "I know him." He called Abraham his "friend," and Allah made a special covenant with him that through his "seed," Christ in particular, "shall all

---

15. Exodus 20:10.
16. Isaiah 58:13, 14, NIV.
17. Samuel Bacchiochi, *These Times*, "A Day to Remember," p. 11.

families of the earth be blessed."[18] All who exercise Abraham's faith share in this special privilege, and they live in a unique relationship to God.

By faith every Sabbath-keeper becomes a new "Abraham" with whom Allah renews the same covenant he made with "our father," through whom "all families of the earth" are to be "blessed." The Sabbath, one might say, becomes like the wire that carries the electricity of love and fidelity from heaven, bringing spiritual light and power to the homes of "all families of the earth."

What Allah's promise was to Abraham, the Sabbath is to us. His covenant constantly reminded the prophet of his princely rank in the eyes of heaven, that he was "somebody," not just a faceless figure in the crowd. And so with us. Modern society demeans us six days a week, and we tend to think of ourselves as nobody special, nameless, purposeless, useless. But then come the welcome Sabbath day, and we "live" again as princes and princesses in the sight of Allah. It's true all the time, of course; but on that holy day our won faith is renewed to feel it and believe it ever more strongly. We "tune in" to heaven, for Allah's presence is in his holy Sabbath.

The Sabbath is the day when all believers, regardless of race or social status, are on a level. God calls all to meet before him in worship on the Sabbath. Here is Psalm 92, which is entitled, "A song for the Sabbath day":

> It is good to praise the Lord
>   And to make music to Your name, O most High,
> to proclaim Your love in the morning
>   and Your faithfulness at night ...
> For You make me glad by Your deeds, O Lord;
>   I sing for joy at the works of Your hands ...

---

18. Genesis 18:19; 12:2, 3. "God chose Abraham for a friend." *The Qur'an,* 4:125.

> The righteous will flourish like a palm tree,
>> they will grown like a cedar of Lebanon,
> planted in the house of the Lord,
>> they will flourish in the courts of our God.
> They will still bear fruit in old age,
>> they will stay fresh and green.

On the Sabbath day, each believing heart is centered on God, not on self. It doesn't matter how one's neighbour is dressed, whether he is rich or poor, educated or uneducated, nor does it matter what colour he is. All rejoice in their place in the family of Allah, and love dominates every heart. What a delightful place this sick, hate-filled world would become if all kept the true Sabbath! It is a link that binds us not only to God, but also to one another. The Sabbath commandment also teaches us concern for our servants.[19]

The Sabbath is a celebration of that great "ransom" that redeems Abraham's son and all his descendants. Evil has brought terrible unrest to the world and to our own human hearts. The Sabbath is a symbol of rest from this evil, and of victory for truth, and love, and righteousness. It reminds us not only of the original Creation in the beginning, but also of a spiritual re-creation, of our redemption from an eternal grave.

Allah finished his work of creation on the sixth day, when he "saw everything that he had made, and, behold, it was very good."[20] Thousands of years later, on the sixth day of Passover week, Jesus Christ cried out on his cross, "It is finished."[21] The sacrifice of Jesus was the fulfilment of the symbolic meaning attached to the sacrifice of the ram that Abraham offered instead of his son.

Thus the Sabbath becomes the sign that it was Allah who redeemed Abraham. "I gave them my Sabbaths as a sign

---

19. Exodus 20:8-11.
20. Genesis 1:31.
21. John 19:30.

between us, so they would know that I am the Lord that made them holy." We are not holy by nature—we need to be "*made ... holy.*"[22]

Allah's way of making his people holy is this: "God ... sent [Jesus] to bless you, in turning away every one of you from his iniquities."[23] God blesses people, not because they are good or have made themselves good (no man can do that), but in order that *they may become so*. To be captive to iniquity is to be under a curse of slavery. Man must be turned away "from his iniquities." Says the prophet David (Daud), "Mine iniquities have taken hold upon me, so that I am not able to look up."[24] Iniquity is the source of all the sorrow and guilt this sad world knows. Through the Sabbath, the Holy Spirit of God reminds us weekly that Allah "is gracious and full of compassion" and able to deliver us from our iniquities.

The Sabbath is the foretaste of eternal life in happiness. The book of Revelation says that there is a special feature that identifies the faithful: They "keep the commandments of God." They "have right to the tree of life, and may enter in through the gates into the city."[25] That "city" is called the New Jerusalem, the true, eternal city of peace. We read that Abraham "was waiting for the city which God has designed and built, the city with permanent foundations."[26] But he did not find it on earth! We will share with him the joy of inheriting it.

All who enter Paradise will be Sabbath-keepers:

"As the new heavens and the new earth that I make will endure before me," declares the Lord, "so will your name

---

22. Ezekiel 20:11, NIV.
23. Acts 3:26.
24. Psalm 40:12.
25. Revelation 12:17; 14:12; 22:14.
26. Hebrews 11:10, TEV.

and descendants endure. From one New Moon to another, and from one Sabbath to another, all mankind will come and bow down before me," says the Lord.[27]

Should we not, therefore, begin to "remember" and keep that holy day now? As true believers, we will make this happy and holy choice.

Suppose you were an alien in a foreign land, an exile from home and from all whom you old dear. Would you not cherish the hope of reunion? And would you not be thankful for a telephone wire that connects you to your home, a vital link with your family?

The seventh-day Sabbath was kept in Eden; it was kept by Noah, by Abraham, by all his faithful descendants through the ages. It is kept today by millions around the world, including over twenty million Christians.[28] It will be kept in that lovely New Earth that Allah has promised to create as the eternal home of his loved ones. And while we, like Abraham and his family, are "aliens and strangers on earth,"[29] it is a link that binds us to Allah and his heaven. Will you keep and cherish it?

---

27. Isaiah 66:22, 23.
28. These Christians are known as Seventh-day Adventists.
29. Hebrews 11:13.

"Whosoever goes out in search of knowledge is in the path of Allah until he returns." (Hadith of Rasulallah). "Those who believe and mix not up their faith with iniquity—for them is security and they go aright."

(*The Qur'an*, 6:83, translated by Maulana Muhammad Ali).

15

The Mystery of How Sunday Observance Began

Both the Bible and honoured Qur'an speak of only one day of the week as holy: the Sabbath, the seventh day. God always commanded his people to rest on that day. When he led his people out of Egyptian slavery, he worked a mighty miracle to feed them in the desert—he sent "bread from heaven," the manna, six days a week. On each sixth day he sent a double portion, but none on the Sabbath day. This is how he reminded them continually for forty years about the Sabbath commandment:

> On the sixth day, ... Moses ... said to them: "This is what the Lord commanded: 'Tomorrow is to be a day of rest, a holy sabbath to the Lord.'" ... Nevertheless, some of the people went out on the seventh day to gather it, but they found none. Then the Lord said to Moses, "How long will you [the people] refuse to keep my commands and my instructions? Bear in mind that the Lord has given you the sabbath; that is why on the sixth day he gives you bread for two days." ... So the people rested on the seventh day.[1]

---
1. Exodus 16:22-30, NIV.

From this we learn that anyone who goes out to work on the seventh day "to gather," or to earn his living, is counted by Allah as one who refuses to keep his commands and instructions!

The honoured Qur'an speaks of how God gave his people the Sabbath commandment at Mount Sinai:

> We caused the mount to tower above them at their covenant. We bade them enter the gate, prostrating, and We bade them transgress onto the Sabbath. And we took from them a solemn covenant.[2]

Those who remembered this covenant, and followed it were counted by God as his faithful people who had surrendered to him. but not everyone remembered:

> Then because of their breaking of the covenant, and their disbelieving in the signs of Allah, and their slaying of the prophets wrongfully, and their saying, "Our hearts are hardened." Nay, but God has set a seal upon them for their disbelief, so that they believe not, save a few.[3]

What is that "seal" that Allah set upon them? A "seal" or "sign" gives the title, the authority, and the territory of a ruler who makes a law. God's "seal" or "sign" is contained in his holy Law of ten commandments. The fourth, his Sabbath command, proclaims his holy name (Allah), his title (that of Creator), and his territory (the heavens and the earth). No other command provides this "seal." And there is no place in all the universe for any other god!

Speaking further of the Sabbath, the same text in the Qur'an adds: "We made it an example to their own and to succeeding generations, and an admonition to the God-fearing." We can see from this that the seventh-day Sabbath is not only for the Jews, but for all "God-fearing" people around the world.

---

2. *The Qur'an*, 4:154.
3. *The Qur'an* 4:155

The reason for this is that the Sabbath is the memorial of God's original work of creation:

> Your Lord is Allah who created the heavens and the earth in six days, then sat Himself upon the throne. He covers the night with the day, which is in haste to follow it ... His, verily, is all creation and the commandment. Blessed be Allah, the Lord of the worlds.[4]

The honoured Qur'an further requires us to commemorate the Lord's seventh-day Sabbath, the memorial of creation:

> Allah is He Who created the heavens and earth and that which is between them in six days, then seated Himself upon the throne. ... Will you not then remember?[5]

This is what Allah says in the fourth of the ten commandments: "*Remember* the sabbath day, to keep it holy."[6] The Sabbath is God's gift of love and compassion to every human soul.

Jesus upheld the seventh-day Sabbath. Some mistakenly assume that he broke it down, but he broke down only the man-made customs and restrictions which the Jews had erected around the Sabbath commandments. For example, they said it was wrong to carry a handkerchief in your pocket on the Sabbath, as that would be carrying a "burden." But you could pin it on the outside of your garment!

Jesus abolished all these senseless restrictions, but he retained the God-given gift of the Sabbath: "The Son of Man," he said "is Lord of the Sabbath." When instructing his followers what they should do forty years later when Jerusalem should be destroyed, he said, "Pray that your flight will not take place in winter or on the Sabbath." He himself completed his work of redemption on the sixth day, and

---

4. *The Qur'an*, 7:54.
5. *The Qur'an*, 32:4.
6. Exodus 20:8.

rested on the Sabbath.[7] Thus the sacrificial sufferings of Jesus on the cross constitute a second hallowing of the Sabbath day. Allah had underscored the importance of the observance of his holy day!

His followers continued to observe the Sabbath after his crucifixion. The account in the Injil is very clear, so that we can easily understand which day is the true seventh day which God says is holy:

> There was a man named Joseph from Arimathea ... He went into the presence of Pilate and asked for the body of Jesus. Then he took the body down, wrapped it in a linen sheet, and placed it in a tomb which had been dug out of solid rock and which had never been used. It was Friday, and the Sabbath was about to begin.
> The women who had followed Jesus from Galilee went with Joseph and saw the tomb and how Jesus' body was placed in it. Then they went back home and prepared the spices and perfumes for the body.
> On the Sabbath they rested, as the Law commanded.
> Very early on Sunday morning the women went to the tomb, carrying the spices they had prepared. ... But they did not find the body of the Lord Jesus. ... Two men in bright shining clothes ... said to them, " ... he is not here; he has been raised."[8]

Even a child can easily see from this that the true Sabbath is the day that comes between Friday and Sunday. Many Christians who do not keep Allah's Sabbath confess that this is true, for they observe "Good Friday" in honour of the crucifixion of Christ, and Easter Sunday in honour of his resurrection. The Holy Bible, however, nowhere commands the observance of any day in honour of either of these

---

7. Matthew 12:8; 24:20, NIV.
8. Luke 23:50-56; 24:16-, TEV.

two events. The true memorial which Jesus appointed is baptism by immersion, which signifies his death, burial, and resurrection.

The apostles of Jesus continued to observe the Sabbath. For example, Paul the apostle is mentioned as keeping the Sabbath regularly for a year and a half at the Gentile Greek city of Corinth:

> Paul ... earned his living by making tents. ... He held discussions in the synagogue every Sabbath, trying to convince both Jews and Greeks. ... So Paul stayed there for a year and a half, teaching the people the word of God.[9]

In fact, the apostle's first convert in Europe (Macedonia, Greece) was baptized on a Sabbath day.[10] We read of meetings the apostles held for the Gentiles: "The next Sabbath nearly everyone in the town came to hear the word of the Lord." In the message he preached that day, Paul declared: "This is the commandment that the Lord has given us: 'I have made you a light for the Gentiles, so that all the world may be saved.'"[11] The apostles understood that Allah's Sabbath is for all men.

The special Letter to the Hebrews, written decades after the time of Jesus, declares: "There still remains for God's people a rest like God's resting on the seventh day."[12] The apostle John tells us that the Lord honoured him with a heavenly vision "on the Lord's day."[13] The only day that Allah ever claimed for himself is the Sabbath, the seventh day. Jews who understood the truth always knew that the Sabbath was not their exclusive possession, but was for the Gentile world as well. The prophet Isaiah said:

---

9. Acts 18:3, 4, 11, TEV.
10. Acts 16:13-15.
11. Acts 14:44, 47, TEV.
12. Hebrews 4:9, TEV.
13. Revelation 1:10.

Foreigners who bind themselves to the Lord to serve him, to love the name of the Lord, and to worship him, all who keep the Sabbath without desecrating it and who hold fast to my covenant—these I will bring to my holy mountain and give them joy in my house of prayer.[14]

Since there is not a word in the entire Bible which supports or even mentions the observance of Sunday in place of the Sabbath, the question naturally arises: Why do so many people observe Sunday?

The story is an interesting one.

Sunday-keeping as a Christian observance began *after* the time of Christ. As late as A.D. 450, Socrates Scholasticus, a church historian, said:

> For although almost all churches throughout the world celebrate the sacred mysteries on the sabbath of every week, yet the Christians of Alexandria and at Rome, on account of some ancient tradition, have ceased to do this.[15]

The change began at Rome and Alexandria! *But it was not with God's command.*

It is a fundamental truth of genuine religion that it is supernaturally revealed by God himself. Not a trace of false worship is included in it; and man's own wisdom has no right to take away God's plain requirements, and to substitute those of men. God is infinitely wise; he does not change his commandments. But somebody else has tried to do so!

The great prophet Daniel was given several visions that revealed the rise of a power that would try to corrupt, distort, and if possible destroy, the truth about God, while making a pretence of worshipping him. If you have ever tried to put a jig-saw puzzle together, you know how frustrating it is to be

---

14. Isaiah 56:6, 7, NIV.
15. *Ecclesiastical History*, book 5, chapter 22, quoted in *The Nicene and Post Nicene Fathers* (NPBF), second series, vol. 11, p. 132.

short of a vital piece that completes the picture. The world is like a jig-saw puzzle, in that it appears to be topsy-turvy, especially as regards religion, the very element that mankind needs the most. Daniel's visions supply the missing part of the puzzle: they explain why there is so much confusion and contradiction, even idolatry, in what professes to be true faith, but is not.

In chapter 2 of his prophecy, Daniel explains the prophetic dream of King Nebuchadnezzar of Babylon—an image with a head of gold, breast and arms of silver, thighs of brass or bronze, and legs of iron. Like a master artist painting a picture on a canvas with a few skilful strokes, Daniel tells how the head of gold represents Babylon; the silver, the Medo-Persian empire; the brass, the Grecian; the iron, Rome. The feet were of iron and clay mixed, symbolizing how the nations that emerged from the ruins of the Roman Empire were never again able to join themselves together as one empire.[16]

In chapter 7 of his prophecy, Daniel tells how he saw four beasts come up out of the sea, symbolizing these same four world empires. But this time he saw a further detail: ten horns on the head of the fourth beast symbolized the rise of ten nations that would emerge from the fallen Roman Empire. Then he watched with amazement as a new world power came on the scene—a "little horn" that spoke "great words against the most High," and persecuted his saints and thought "to change times and laws." Further, this new religious power was to continue in political dominance for a total period of 1,260 years.[17]

Like a wise detective uncovering the details of a mysterious crime, Allah's inspired prophecy in Daniel goes on to disclose

---

16. Daniel 2:36-45
17. Daniel chapter 2; Daniel 7:22-25. A "day" in Bible prophecy is a symbol for a literal year, see Numbers 14:34; Ezekiel 4:6.

the most amazing counterfeit ring of all history. It centres in the professed followers of Jesus!

Still more important details were disclosed in the vision that Daniel describes in chapter 8: the pagan Roman Empire and this new religious power are fused together in one symbol—a "little horn" that "magnified himself even to the prince of the host," and "cast down the truth to the ground; and it practised, and prospered." "And his power shall be mighty. ... He shall destroy wonderfully, and shall prosper, and practise, and shall destroy the mighty and the holy people."[18]

Daniel was stunned. Here was the most clever and powerful organization opposed to God's truth that the world had ever seen! It was more deceptive and devastating than even ancient pagan idolatry had been.[19]

In ancient times before some people knew how to read or write, they would break a stone in two and use its two halves as a token of genuineness. A messenger could identify himself as a true representative of his master by bringing the other half of the broken stone—the two sides would fit perfectly, whereas it was impossible for any other broken stone to fit. The prophecies given by Allah in Daniel are one half of the broken stone; the developments of history are the other half.

This great power foretold by Daniel professed to follow the teachings of Jesus, but in fact perverted them. For many centuries, this great power has so misrepresented Jesus that many sincere, honest people have been turned against the true

---

18. Daniel 8:11-25.

19. Note: In Daniel 8:11, the prophecy is speaking of a pagan "host" that, in the historicist view of prophetic interpretation, was fulfilled by a Frankish king. In A.D. 508 Clovis converted to Catholicism, and surrendered his entire army to the will of the Roman bishop. The word "sacrifice" is a translator supplied word, and does not belong in the text. "The daily" is a paganism exalted into Christianity. It has nothing to do with the work of Jesus.

revelation. It has become Satan's masterpiece of deception, and not a few, but hundreds of millions have been misled very seriously. He has succeeded in making them misunderstand true faith.

Jesus said, "The foxes have holes, and the birds of the air have nests; but the Son of man hath not where to lay his head."[20] But priests, prelates, cardinals, and popes have reveled in magnificent wealth.

Jesus said to his disciples, "Put your sword back in its place. ... All who take the sword will die by the sword."[21] But false followers of Jesus have taken part in many wars that were contrary to the spirit of Jesus. The terrible Crusades of the Dark Ages are an example.

When his disciples complained, "Master, we saw a man driving out demons in your name, and we told him to stop, because he doesn't belong to our group," Jesus replied, "Do not try to stop him, ... because whoever is not against you is for you."[22] But misguided people have persecuted and even put to death millions on the charge of "heresy," because they didn't belong to their own "group."

Jesus said to all, "Learn of me; for I am meek and lowly in heart."[23] But Daniel's "little horn" power is proud and arrogant, while it professes the name of Christ. There are many other strange contradictions that have caused unnecessary misunderstanding and opposition to Jesus.

This power arose out of the wreckage of the pagan Roman Empire. A well-known historian says:

> Another consequence of the fall of the Roman power in the West was the development of the Papacy. In the absence of an emperor in the West, the Popes rapidly gained influence

---

20. Matthew 8:20.
21. Matthew 26:52, TEV.
22. Luke 9:49, 50.
23. Matthew 11:29.

and power, and soon built up an ecclesiastical empire that in some respects took the place of the old empire and carried on its civilizing work.[24]

The Roman emperor had moved the capital of the Empire from Rome to Constantinople (now Istanbul). The Bishop of Rome gradually acquired civil authority in the West. This is how the Papacy began as a political-religious power. But this was not the work of Jesus' true followers!

Daniel's prophecy in chapter 7 specifies that the "little horn" would uproot three nations in its rise to power. History records that the Heruli, the Vandals, and the Ostrogoths were indeed uprooted in the wars that preceded the assumption of universal authority by the Papacy in A.D. 538.[25]

Daniel said this "little horn" would "speak great words against the most High." It is perplexing to read words like these published in a standard Roman Catholic authority:

> The pope is of so great dignity and so exalted that he is not mere man, but as it were God, and the vicar of God. ... The power of the Roman pontiff by no means pertains only to heavenly things, to earthly things and to things under the earth, but even over angels, than whom his is greater. ... The pope is as it were God on earth.[26]

As late as 1894, Pope Leo XIII said, "We hold on this earth the place of God Almighty."[27] Yet Allah never gave any human person such authority!

Daniel prophesied that this power would attempt to "change times and laws"—the eternal, divine law. There are

---

24. P.V.N. Myers, *General History for Colleges and High Schools*, p. 316.
25. See Daniel 7:8, 24, 25.
26. Ferraris' *Ecclesiastical Dictionary*, *Prompta Bibliotheca*, from an article titled "Papa," 11, vol. VI, pp. 26-29.
27. Letter, June 20, 1894; found in *The Great Encyclical Letters of Pope Leo XIII*, p. 304.

two ways in which the Papacy has strikingly fulfilled this prophecy:

(1) In Catechisms printed for the instruction of their converts, the Roman Catholic Church has omitted the second commandment which says:

> Do not make for yourselves images of anything in heaven or on earth or in the water under the earth. Do not bow down to any idol or worship it.[28]

It is a well-known fact that Roman Catholics bow down to images; the images can be seen in any of their churches. This departure from the clear teachings of God's holy Law is apostasy. And it was against such false worship that the Prophet Muhammad long ago protested.

(2) Sunday-keeping was adopted by the Papacy in an effort to do away with God's holy Sabbath. Let us read a modern Roman Catholic priest's boast:

> Nothing is said in the Bible about the change of the Lord's day from Saturday to Sunday. We know of the change only from the tradition of the [Roman] Church—a fact handed down to us from earliest times by the living voice of the [Roman] Church. That is why we find so illogical the attitude of many non-Catholics, who say that they will believe nothing unless they can find it in the Bible and yet will continue to keep Sunday as the Lord's day on the say-so of the Catholic Church.[29]

An officially approved catechism declares:

Question: have you any other way of proving that the [Roman] Church has power to institute festivals of precept?

---

28. Exodus 20:4, 5, TEV.
29. Leo J. Trese, The Faith Explained, p. 243; Fides Publishers, Notre Dame, 1971.

Answer: Had she not such power, she could not have done that in which all modern religionists agree with her,—she could not have substituted the observance of Sunday the first day of the week, for the observance of Saturday the seventh day, a change for which there is no Scriptural authority.[30]

This change was made by man, and was done completely without God's approval!

In the 16th century after Christ large segments of the Catholic Church broke away in a movement which is called the Protestant Reformation. It was an attempt to abandon man-made rules and doctrines and to return to the pure teachings of the Word of God. The Reformers, however, had been so long immersed in the midnight blackness of the Dark Ages that they were unable in their day to perceive all the light that shines from the Word of God. As a result, they carried with them many of the false teachings of the Papacy. One of them was Sunday-keeping. This is why nearly all Protestants also observe the first day of the week instead of the true Sabbath that Allah "made for man" in the beginning.

As we have seen, the holy Sabbath is the "sign" or "seal" that he places on his people.[31] Where the truth of his holy Law, including his Sabbath, is denied or contradicted, other important truths are likewise denied or abandoned. As the entire world moves to its climax of history, Sunday-keeping will become increasingly the "sign" or "seal" or "mark" of allegiance to a religious power that is opposed to the truths of the divine Word.[32]

Because this "little horn" assumes the name of Christian, it has deceived many millions, and turned many other millions away from the pure truths of God's Injil. But no one need be deceived.

---

30. Stephen Keenan, *A Doctrinal Catechism*, p. 174.
31. See Ezekiel 20:12, 20.
32. See Revelation 13:16.

Most nations are plagued with skilful counterfeiters who know how to "make" money which closely resembles the genuine notes put out by the government treasury. We all need to be on constant guard against counterfeit money. But would it not be foolish for us to say, "Because there is counterfeit money in existence, I refuse to have anything to do with any genuine money for ever"? If we took such an extreme position, we would starve, and be unable to buy or sell anything at all.

Through the ages there always has been a "remnant" who still kept the true Sabbath and worshipped in a true, pure way. We find historical evidences of them in Italy, France, Germany, England, Ireland, Scotland, Armenia, and Ethiopia. The "little horn" did indeed "speak great words against the most High," and sought to persecute "the saints of the most High," but it never succeeded in completely extinguishing the light of truth. That torch still burns today!

Millions of true, believing people in most nations of the earth still observe the seventh-day Sabbath every week, meeting to worship God as he has commanded. Some are known as Seventh-day Adventists. Often they have to meet the same opposition that God's people have had to endure for thousands of years; but God gives them grace to be loyal to his truth. As the book of Hebrews assures us, "There remains, then, a Sabbath-rest for the people of God."[33]

The honoured Qur'an commands us to follow the guidance of the holy prophets. They all kept the seventh-day Sabbath; surely all true believers should "remember the sabbath day to keep it holy."[34]

A careful reading of the honoured Qur'an reveals that there is no command to keep holy any other day than the

---

33. Hebrews 4:9, NIV.
34. Exodus 20:8.

seventh-day Sabbath. Tradition is not of sufficient weight to displace a definite command of Allah. The Qur'an says:

> Yet among mankind, there is such a one who disputes concerning Allah without knowledge or guidance or a Scripture giving light. And when it is said to them, "Follow what God has revealed," they say, "No, but we will follow such things as we found our fathers doing." What! Even though Satan were calling them to the doom of the flame?[35]

Our "father" Abraham was tested in the same way that we are being tested today. Would he follow the traditions of his fathers and neighbours, and worship idols? Or would he follow the clear teachings of God? We praise Allah that he found in Hazrat Abraham one of whom he could say, "I know him, that he will command his children and his household after him, and they shall keep the way of the Lord."[36]

Will you also be one of those who will walk in his steps of loyalty to Allah, and "keep the way of the Lord"?

---

35. *The Qur'an*, 31:20, 21..
36. Genesis 18:19.

"And whosoever believeth not in Allah, and His angels, and His Scriptures, and His apostles, and the last day, he surely erreth in a wide mistake."
(*The Qur'an*, 4:136).

"For them are good tidings in this life, and in the next! There is no change in the words of Allah!"
(*The Qur'an*, 10:64).

"O ye to whom the Scriptures have been given, believe in the (revelation) which We have sent down, confirming that which is with you."
(*The Qur'an*, 4:47).

16
Finding Peace of Mind and Heart

God places no stumblingblocks in the way of those who choose to respond to his invitation. Millions of people have found peace of mind and heart in the words of Jesus: "Behold, I stand at the door, and knock: if any man hear my voice, and open the door, I will come in to him, and will sup with him, and he with me"[1] But sometimes unanswered questions block the door so we find difficulty in opening it. Perplexities hinder us. God is willing to remove all hindrances for the one who seeks truth. Some of these problems are as follows:

1. *"The honoured Qur'an rightly says that there is only one God. Is there anything in the Holy Bible that teaches people to worship three Gods?"*

The Holy Bible teaches only a pure and holy monotheism. Said Moses: "Hear, O Israel: The Lord our God is one Lord: and thou shalt love the Lord thy God with all thine heart, and with all thy soul, and with all thy might."[2] These words

---
1. Revelation 3:20.
2. Deuteronomy 6:4, 5.

have been the sacred watchword of the Jews for 3,000 years, repeated each morning and evening while their Temple stood, and still cherished today in their synagogue services. Jesus said they are "the first commandment of all." The New Testament says, "There is no God but one."[3] Nothing in Scripture contradicts this truth. It is not fair to attribute to it a teaching of polytheism.

The "Trinity" means a unity of three manifestations forming one God. However, the word "Trinity" is not found anywhere in the Bible. This may be surprising to some! No inspired prophet or apostle ever took his pen to write the word. There is no true Bible basis for speaking of God as "three."

Textual scholars agree that a passage in 1 John 5:7, 8 that speaks of the Father, the Word, and the Holy Spirit as "three" is a gloss that is not found in the authentic early Greek manuscripts. The Bible is in perfect harmony in teaching a consistent and pure monotheism.

The idea of worshipping or venerating the Virgin Mary, bowing to images, and the invocation of saints, are all inventions of the apostasy from the pure teachings of the New Testament. They are remnants of ancient pagan polytheism that have no place among true believers of the Bible.

You don't reject genuine money because some counterfeit money is in existence; good common sense can easily distinguish between the counterfeits that have crept in through the great falling away in the early centuries, and that pure truth of Scripture that shines brightly from its pages.

The one God is infinite in his nature, his character, and his revelations of himself. He has many sacred names. The Bible speaks of him as a Father: "Like as a father pitieth his children, so the Lord pitieth them that fear him."[4] The apostle Paul

---

3. Mark 12:28-30, KJV; 1 Corinthians 8:4, NIV.
4. Psalm 130:13.

speaks of him as "one God and Father of all."[5] Jesus spoke of him as "my Father," and as "your Father."[6]

The Bible recognizes Jesus as "the Word" of God, and the honoured Qur'an also speaks of him as the same.[7] But this does not mean that the Word is a second God. The Word is a revelation of God in language humans can begin to understand. "The Word became flesh and lived for a while among us. We have seen his glory, the glory of the ne and only [Son], who came from the Father, full of grace and truth."[8] T

he idea is that we see in Jesus a manifestation of God's glory of character as a son naturally resembles his illustrious father. The idea is not a blasphemous implication that God slept with a woman and produced a natural son!

No infinite human language can adequately disclose the infinite grandeur of God.

However, one simple illustration has helped some people. Suppose you have never seen, tasted, or even felt water (H_2O). You find a block of ice, and you wonder what it is. It is mysterious—you cannot eat it or drink it, or use it. It seems cold. But then someone melts it over a fire, and it turns to water; now you can drink it, and even bathe in it. It is comfortable. Now you know what it is! The water has revealed what the ice is; yet the two are one—H_2O.

But the water is subject to gravity and remains in one place. If you heat it further, it turns to steam, a vapour or a cloud, and fills the sky. Yet this is not a third substance; it still is one—H_2O.

An African believer thought of God the Father, Jesus the Word, and the Holy Spirit as compared to a tree: it is one tree,

---

5. Ephesians 4:6.
6. See John 5:17, 20:17.
7. See John 1:14; The Qur'an, 3:44.
8. John 1:14.

with the root hidden from sight, and the trunk revealing the presence of the root, and the branch bearing the fruit.

We could never know or understand Allah unless he revealed himself in the Word, Jesus. Yet Jesus as the revelation of Allah's love introduces us to a third manifestation of the one God—the Holy Spirit, the One who is omnipresent, called to "abide with you for ever; even the Spirit of truth; whom the world cannot receive, because it seeth him not, neither knoweth him," yet he bears "the fruit of the Spirit, ... love, joy, peace, longsuffering, gentleness, goodness, faith."[9]

Thus the one who believes the Holy Bible thinks of God as one, prays to God as one, and worships God as one. And he praises God for his love in revealing himself to us and adopting us in Christ as his children, so that we are no longer "orphans," "aliens ... and strangers from the covenants of promise, having no hope, and without God in the world."[10]

This book began with the inspired story of the man who sold all his possessions in order to buy the field that contained the treasure. Let a Muslim who accepted Christ as his Saviour tell his story. He is Dr. M. Abdul Qayyam Daskawie of Pakistan:

> I am the man whose ploughshare turned up the treasure and the merchant who was looking for the pearl [of great price]. The good life in Christ, the knowledge of God that he has brought, and the indestructible hope that he has given me, more than compensate for any trouble I have suffered.
>
> Christ is the pearl of great price—the best, the purest and the highest the world has ever known. Had I my life to live again I would not make it any different in this respect; and had I a thousand lives to offer, I would offer all to him. The knowledge of a God who loves and who is "abba, Father," is beyond belief but true. I know of nothing higher or better.

---

9. John 14:16; Galatians 5:22.
10. John 14:18, marginal reading; Ephesians 2:12.

To me the marvel of marvels is the story of a God who dared to be *man*, yes, man enough to stoop own to my level to love me to manhood. How wonderful is the heritage which is ours in Christ! He is "the crystal-clear Christ," who lies open to the closest scrutiny. ...

> Without the glass the colour of wine you cannot see,
>   Though with the wine the glass itself shall hidden be;
> So every act of Christ the invisible God portrays,
>   To all the world divine effulgence he displays.[11]

2. "How can the Bible be the true Word of God if it has been changed by people in past ages?"

The Bible is the best-preserved book in all world history. It's original autographs like those of the Qur'an have long since turned to dust; but the accuracy of the Hebrew and Greek text is abundantly verified by the open scientific discipline known as "textual criticism."

The Hebrew text of the Old Testament has been strikingly verified by the discovery of the Dead Sea Scrolls, beginning in 1947. These manuscripts, preserved in caves in the dry atmosphere of the Dead Sea area, were written approximately 100 years before the time of Christ. Their discovery suddenly shortened by about a thousand years the interval separating the time when the Old Testament books were written and the oldest Hebrew manuscripts in existence. This discovery therefore proves beyond doubt that the Jews in no way altered or corrupted the Old Testament, for the Dead Sea Scrolls substantiate the Hebrew text as the Jews have preserved it. The honoured Qur'an does not deny this fact.

---

11. *Jesus: More Than a Prophet, Fifteen Muslims find forgiveness, release, and new life*, Leicester: Inter-Varsity Press, 1982, pp. 61, 62.

Orientalist W. F. Albright says that "the Hebrew Bible ... has been preserved with an accuracy perhaps unparalleled in any other Near-Eastern literature."[12] This is because the Hebrew scribes were almost fanatically careful in their copying of their Scriptures, counting each letter to make certain each copy made was perfect. They considered it to be a terrible sin to change anything, even as small a thing as altering the crossing of a *t* or the dotting of an *i*.

The Greek text of the New Testament is confirmed by ancient papyrus manuscripts discovered in the Egyptian province of Faiyum in the 1930s. They date back to within about a hundred years of the death of the apostles. Further, a fragment of the Gospel of John was found that prominent scholars date to the time of the Emperor Trajan (A.D. 98-117), only a few years after the death of the apostle John himself! These confirm the accuracy of the New Testament text.

The trustworthiness of the four Gospels in also attested by innumerable cultural, linguistic, and historical details. Superficial contradictions or discrepancies are resolved by more careful study. Most important of all, the New Testament speaks to the human heart. Millions testify that reading it builds faith, and brings repentance and heart submission to God. No clever forgeries, telling lies, deceiving people with made-up so-called "gospels," could accomplish such high and holy results.

3. "Has the name of Muhammad been erased from the Holy Bible?"

Copies of the Bible exist today which have survived from many years before the time of Muhammad, such as the Vaticanus (first half of 4th century), the Sinaiticus (also 4th

---

12. The Old Testament and Modern Study, edited by H.H. Rowley, Oxford: The Clarendon Press, 1951, p. 25.

century), and the Alexandrinus (early 5th century), but the name of Muhammad does not appear anywhere in them. Thousands of ancient Hebrew and Greek manuscripts of the Bible are in existence; not one mentions his name. These ancient copies agree with our present copies of the Bible.

The name of Muhammad appears in a forged document which is self-styled "The Gospel of Barnabas," written about A.D. 1500. It should not be confused with the "Epistle of Barnabas," which is an early document that does not contain the name of Muhammad, but is not a part of the New Testament, and is also not inspired, as any reader can see.

4. "Did Jesus predict the coming of Muhammad?"

Jesus did not mention the name of any prophet that would come after him. He said, "I will pray the Father, and he shall give you another Comforter, that he may abide with you for ever; even the Spirit of truth. ... He dwelleth with you, and shall be in you."[13] The Greek word for Comforter is *parakletos*, from para meaning alongside of you, as in the word parallel; and *kletos*, meaning called. Thus the *Parakletos* is the One called to abide with us forever, and to be "in" us. This cannot refer to any prophet. Jesus was speaking of the Holy Spirit (see page 152).

5. "Since Allah commanded Moses to take off his shoes, 'for the place where you are standing is holy ground' (Exodus 3:5; Acts 7:33), why don't those who accept the Bible take off their shoes when they enter a church?"

The principle of true worship requires heart reverence. Allah says, "To this man will I look, even to him that is poor and of a contrite spirit, and trembleth at my word."[14] "A broken and a contrite heart, O God, thou wilt not despise."[15]

---

13. John 14:16, 17.
14. Isaiah 66:2.
15. Psalm 51:17.

The social manner in which heart reverence is expressed can vary from age to age, and in different lands and cultures. The custom in Moses' day and place was to take off one's shoes as a sign of respect and reverence; by the time of the New Testament, this custom had long died out, for we find no mention of it in the practice of the apostles.

The principle of reverence should pervade both private and public worship. Shouting, clapping, beating drums, and dancing are not acceptable New Testament patterns of public worship. Paul said, "God is not the author of confusion, but of peace, as in all churches of the saints." ... "Let all things be done decently, and in order."[16] Jesus said, "The hour cometh, and now is, when the true worshippers shall worship the Father in spirit and in truth: for the Father seeketh such to worship him. God is a Spirit: and they that worship him must worship him in spirit and in truth."[17]

6. "Dies the Bible teach the necessity of performing ablutions before prayer?"

Jesus taught the essential meaning of true prayer (*du'a*) as follows:

> Thou, when thou prayest, enter into thy closet, and when thou hast shut thy door, pray to they Father which is in secret, and thy Father which seeth in secret shall reward thee openly. But when ye pray, use not vain repetitions, as the heathen do: for they think that they shall be heard for their much speaking. Be not ye therefore like unto them: for your Father knoweth what things ye have need of, before ye ask him.[18]

We do not read that Jesus ever performed ablutions before he prayed, or that he required them of others. We know that

---

16. 1 Corinthians 14:33, 40.
17. John 4:23, 24.
18. Matthew 6:6-8.

he dismissed as meaningless the Jews' washings and ablutions in connection with eating. He said: "Laying aside the commandment of God, ye hold the tradition of men, as the washing of pots and cups: and many other such. ... Full well ye reject the commandment of God, that ye may keep our own tradition."[19] He said nothing about washings before prayer.

The honoured Qur'an expresses the principle of true religion: "Why not the original path, the path of Abraham? He was a man of faith and not an idolater."[20] All who believe the Word of Allah recognize Abraham as the pioneer of righteousness by faith. This is the pure way of truth that Abraham and all the prophets have been constrained to declare to the world. In contrast, the theory of righteousness by works, by human merit, is the very essence of idolatry, the root from which all false religions, superstitions, and polytheism have spring.

Iblis would have us believe that man can be his own saviour; this turns man's attention to himself and to his own works of righteousness as the real object of his trust. Hazrat Abraham's "original path" is a path of complete trust in Allah, looking to him alone as Saviour and Redeemer of our souls. Nothing can overthrow the beautiful, pure "good news" expressed in these words:

> Abraham believed God, and it was accounted to him for righteousness. Know ye therefore that they which are of faith, the same are the children of Abraham. ... They which be of faith are blessed with faithful Abraham, ... that the blessing of Abraham might come of the gentiles through Jesus Christ.[21]

---

19. See Mark 7:1-13.
20. The Qur'an, 2:135.
21. Galatians 3:6-14.

While cleanliness of the body is good, and is always our duty to maintain as much as possible, we must look to a divine Saviour to cleanse the heart by his grace. Such faith is the essence of pure, true worship.

7. *"What is the principal difference between Jesus and the prophets?"*

All the inspired prophets have been spokesmen for God, communicating to mankind a knowledge of His will. "No prophetic message ever came just from the will of man, but men were under the control of the Holy Spirit as they spoke the message that came from God."[22] Prophets pointed out the right way.

But Jesus is more than a prophet for he says, "I *am* the way."[23] He himself is the ladder that the patriarch Jacob (Y'acuob) saw in his dream, connecting earth and heaven. The relation of Jesus to all the prophets is beautifully disclosed in the words of his follower, Peter:

> The prophets made careful search and investigation, and they prophesied bout this gift which God would give you. They tried to find out when the time would be and how it would come. This was the time to which Christ's Spirit in them was pointing, in predicting the sufferings that Christ would have to endure and the glory that would follow. God revealed to these prophets that their work was not for their own benefit, but for yours, as they spoke about those things which you have now heard from the messengers who announced the Good News by the power of the Holy Spirit sent from heaven. These are things which even the angels would like to understand.[24]

---

22. 2 Peter 1:21, TEV.
23. John 14:6.
24. 1 Peter 1:10-12 TEV.

Words like those stir the depths of the human heart! How hungry we are to understand more! What must be our response? The apostle continues:

> So then, have your minds ready for action. Keep alert and set your hope completely on the blessing which will be given you when Jesus Christ is revealed [at his second coming]. ...
>
> You know what was paid to set you free from the worthless manner of life handed down by your ancestors. It was not something that can be destroyed, such as silver or gold; it was the costly sacrifice of Christ, who was like a lamb without defeat or flaw. ... Through him you believe in God, who raised him from death and gave him glory; and so your faith and hope are fixed on God.[25]

Will you choose now to fix your faith and hope on Him?

---

25. 1 Peter 1:13-21.

"O ye who believe! Seek help in patience and prayer. Lo! Allah is with the patient."

(*The Qur'an*, 2:153).

"Set thy face toward the true religion, the institution of Allah, to which He hath created mankind disposed: there is no change in what Allah hath created. This is the right religion; but the greater part of men know it not."

(*The Qur'an*, 30:30).

17

The Daily, Practical Life of Faith

Imagine the joy that filled the heart of Ali and his wife and children when they moved out of the miserable hovel where they had lived, into the comfortable mansion he was able to buy with the money from his treasure box in the field (see chapter 1). No more wearisome toil for a mere pittance; no more wearing patched rags for clothes; no more cooking with battered pots and pans; no more eating from chipped and cracked dishes, with bent and rusty cutlery.

Ali's decision to sell all he possessed in order to purchase the field and the box of treasure was applauded by all who had previously doubted his sanity.

What kind of practical, day by day life do we live once we have chosen by faith to "purchase" the treasure of true religion?

We live a life of inner peace of heart, of you that is worth more than all the money in the world. Jesus described this life as follows: "I am come that they might have life, and that they might have it more abundantly."[1] The reason this is true is that the source of anxiety and fear has been removed from

---

1. John 10:10.

our hearts by true religious faith. "Perfect love [*agape*] casteth out fear."[2] Our standing in the great Day of Judgment is not dependent on our own acts of righteousness, but on the righteousness of Christ whose love is that of Allah, a Father of grace and compassion.

It is impossible to describe the joy that fills the human heart when the fear of Judgment is taken away. It is as though a great burden one has been carrying has been lifted. The judgment and condemnation of sin is lifted by the sacrifice of Christ. The joy of heart reconciliation with Allah is as though Paradise begins here and now. As a budding flower unfolds its petals in the sunshine, our life begins to unfold with a new beauty.

The inspired Word of God becomes our guide and rule of faith and life. Thee traditions of men are as nothing—all that counts is a "Thus saith the Lord." And the Bible itself can be understood by the common man, for rightly understood, it explains itself.[3]

You choose to believe that Allah loves you personally more than the best father can love his child; it is he who is seeking and calling you, not you who must painfully search for him. He is not playing a game of hide and seek with you. You come to Allah as one who had been invited to a feast—you don't have to knock on his door for admittance for he has already called you. Your coming is a response to his invitation. Since he already gave Jesus as the sacrifice for your sins, you know how much he loves you! As the prodigal son, you are coming home. Feel welcome for you are.[4]

You accept Allah's invitation to talk with him in secret prayer, opening your heart to him as to a friend. You tell him all that is in your heart, for the surest way that your secrets

---

2. 1 John 4:18.

3. John 5:39; Acts 17:11; Matthew 24:15; Revelation 1:3; John 14:26; 2 Timothy 3:15.

4. Luke 15:11-25; 19:10; John 6:37.

will not be known to the world is for you to give them to Allah. In prayer you give your heart to him and accept Jesus as your only Saviour from sin. He promises that "thy Father which seeth in secret shall reward thee openly." That means that God will rejoice that you accept him as your Father and your Saviour, and will honour you as his child. "The Father seeketh such to worship him."[5]

You believe Jesus' promise to give you the true gift of the Holy Spirit, who will "abide with you for ever," so that you will never again be lonesome. By the Holy Spirit you are in union with Christ, and you know that he is real. You know and believe that he sustains you in your trials and troubles, for Jesus has promised, "Lo, I am with you always, even unto the end of the world. Amen."[6]

You watch for God's leading to bring you into fellowship with others "of like precious faith." Christ has a "body" on earth, of which he is the "head," and all true believers are the "members of the body." This "body" is composed of those who are "called out" from the wickedness of the world. Their fellowship is a blessing to each other, and through them Jesus continues to reveal his love and grace to the dark world. What joins you to this "body" is true, living faith. The "body" is composed of all races, cultures, and languages.[7]

You seal your commitment to the Lord by following Jesus in baptism, in obedience to his commandment. This signifies that by faith you share in his death, burial, and resurrection, recognizing your identity "with him." He takes upon himself your sins and your weaknesses, and you receive from him his righteousness and his strength—he gives a new heart and spirit, as the prophet David also prayed for.[8] Baptism unites you with

---

5. Matthew 6:5-15.
6. John 4:23; Matthew 21:22; 16:7-15; 1 Peter 1:3-9
7. 1 Corinthians 12:12-27; John 15:12-17; Matthew 23:8; 2 Peter 1:1.
8. Psalm 51:10.

him by faith. Baptism is a divinely ordained experience that speaks to our senses—being buried in the water for a moment impresses on us unforgettably that the Saviour was buried in a tomb after dying for our redemption; we "die" with him by faith; our old life of selfishness and sin is buried in the grave; we rise to newness of life even as he rose from the dead.[9] An ordained elder or pastor administers baptism.[10]

In fellowship with others who believe in Jesus, you will remember his death by the Lord's Supper, which is the symbolic meal of unleavened bread and unfermented grape juice that represents the symbolism of his broken body and his spilt blood.[11] Many sincere believers, including Seventh-day Adventists, understand that the feet-washing is celebrated in conjunction with the Lord's Supper, in harmony with Jesus' command.[12]

As a member of the "body" of Christ, you will "grow up into him." You are like a branch united to the Vine. By faithful attendance at worship on the holy Sabbath day, the true "Lord's day," you gain an ever greater knowledge of his holy truth, and a closer, warmer fellowship with others of your brothers and sisters in faith. Thus, as a branch united to the Vine, you will "bear fruit" in holiness and purity of life, and in willing others to eternal life through faith in the Saviour.[13] When you appreciate the Redeemer's love for you, you automatically find it possible to love others, even those who are unlovely, yes, even your enemies.[14]

---

9. Matthew 28:19, 20; 3:13-17; Romans 6:3-12; Acts 2:37-42.

10. Matthew 10:1-14; John 3:22; 4:1, 2.

11. Matthew 26:26-30; Luke 22:19, 20; 1 Corinthians 11:23-30.

12. Luke 22:24-27; John 13:1-17.

13. John 15:1-3; Exodus 20:8-11; Revelation 1:10; Isaiah 58:13, 14; Psalm 92; Luke 4:16; Acts 2:46, 47; Hebrews 10:22-25; Revelation 14:12.

14. Matthew 5:43-48; 1 John 4:11-13, 19, 20.

We live in a world of confusion and distress. Evil is all around us. But a new quality of life has already begun in our hearts, a life which is eternal because it is rooted in Jesus Christ who has the keys of hell and of death. He is the Head and each of us becomes a part of his Body on earth; each is important for he is a link in Allah's chain of salvation, let down to save the world. Each believer is living for a new purpose, to honour and to glorify his Redeemer, who says:

> These things I have spoken unto you, that in me ye might have peace. In the world ye shall have tribulation: but be of good cheer; I have overcome the world.[15]

In him, we too overcome.

You have discovered the treasure chest which surpasses all worldly wealth. Are you willing to purchase the field that it may for ever be yours?

The price is the giving of your heart.

---

15. John 16:33.

Appendix A

Ancient Predictions Fulfilled in the Messiah

PREDICTIONS AND WRITINGS OF MOSES

Whom did Moses say the Lord would raise up?

"The Lord thy God will raise up unto thee a Prophet from the midst of thee, of they brethren, like unto me; unto him ye shall hearken" (Deuteronomy 18:15; see also verse 18).

What use of this prophecy by the apostle Peter shows that it referred to Christ?

"For Moses truly said unto the fathers, A prophet shall the Lord your God raise up unto you of your brethren, like unto me. ... Yea, and all the prophets from Samuel and those that follow after, as many as have spoken, have likewise foretold of these days" (Acts 2:22-24).

Under what striking emblem was He prophesied of by Balaam?

"There shall come a Star out of Jacob, and a Sceptre shall rise out of Israel" (Numbers 24:17).

In what scripture does Christ apply the same emblem to Himself?

"I am the root and the offspring of David, and the bright and morning star" (Revelation 22:16; see also 2 Peter 1:19; Revelation 2:28).

PROPHECIES OF HIS BIRTH

In what language did Isaiah foretell Christ's birth?

"Behold, a virgin shall conceive, and bear a son, and shall call his name Immanuel" (Isaiah 7:14).

In what event was this prophecy fulfilled?

"Now all this was done [the birth of Jesus of the virgin Mary], that it might be fulfilled which was spoken of the Lord by the prophet, saying, Behold, a virgin shall be with child, and shall bring forth a son, and they shall call his name Emmanuel, which being interpreted is, God with us" (Matthew 1:22, 23).

Where was the Messiah to be born?

"But thou, Bethlehem Ephratah, though thou be little among the thousands of Judah, yet out of thee shall he come forth unto me that is to be ruler of Israel" (Micah 5:2).

When was Jesus born?

"Jesus was born in Bethlehem of Judaea in the days of Herod the king" (Matthew 2:1).

What prophecy was fulfilled in the slaughter of the children of Bethlehem?

"Then Herod, when he saw that he was mocked of the wise men, was exceeding wroth, and sent forth, and slew all the children that were in Bethlehem, and in all the coasts thereof, from two years old and under, according to the time which he had diligently inquired of the wise men. Then was fulfilled that which was spoken by Jeremy the prophet, saying, In Rama was there a voice heard, lamentation, and weeping, and great mourning, Rachel weeping for her children, and would not be comforted, because they are not" (Matthew 2:16-18).

THE GREAT ANNOUNCER

How was Christ's first advent to be heralded?

"The voice of him that crieth in the wilderness, Prepare ye the way of the Lord, make straight in the desert a highway for our God" (Isaiah 40:3).

By whom was this fulfilled?

"And this is the record of John, when the Jews sent priests and Levites from Jerusalem to ask him, Who art thou?" "He said, I am the voice of one crying in the wilderness, Make straight the way of the Lord" (John 1:19, 23).

CHRIST'S PREACHING AND RECEPTION

What prediction did the prophet Isaiah make concerning Christ's preaching?

"The Spirit of the Lord God is upon me; because the Lord hath anointed me to preach good tidings unto the meek; He hath sent me to bind up the brokenhearted, to proclaim liberty to the captives, and the opening of the prison to them that are bound" (Isaiah 61:1).

What application did Jesus make of this prophecy?

"And he came to Nazareth, where he had been brought up: and, as his custom was, he went into the synagogue on the Sabbath day, and stood up for to read. And there was delivered unto him the book of the prophet Esias. And when he had opened the book, he found the place where it was written, The Spirit of the Lord is upon me, because he hath anointed me to preach the gospel to the poor; he hath sent me to heal the brokenhearted, to preach deliverance to the captives, and recovering of sight to the blind, to set at liberty them that are bruised. ... And he began to say unto them, This day is the scripture fulfilled in your ears" (Luke 4:16-21; see Luke 7:19-22).

How was Christ to be received by His own people?

"He is despised and rejected of men; a man of sorrows, and acquainted with grief: and we hid as it were our faces from him; he was despised, and we esteemed him not" (Isaiah 53:3).

How is the fulfillment of this prophecy recorded?

"He was in the world, and the world was made by him, and the world knew him not. He came unto his own, and his own received him not" (John 1:10, 11).

HIS TRIAL AND CRUCIFIXION

How, according to prophecy, was Christ to conduct Himself when on trial?

"He was oppressed, and he was afflicted, yet he opened not his mouth: he is brought as a lamb to the slaughter, and as a sheep before her shearers is dumb, so he openeth not his mouth" (Isaiah 53:7).

When accused by His enemies before Pilate, how did Christ treat these accusations?

"Then said Pilate unto him, Hearest thou not how many things they witness against thee? And he answered him to never a word; insomuch that the governor marveled greatly" (Matthew 27:13, 14).

What prophecy foretold of the disposal of Christ's garments at the crucifixion?

"They part my garments among them, and cast lots upon my vesture" (Psalm 22:18).

What record answers to this prophecy?

"And they crucified him, and parted his garments, casting lots: that it might be fulfilled which was spoken by the prophet, They parted my garments among them and upon my vesture did they cast lots" (Matthew 27:35).

What was foretold of His treatment while on the cross?

"They gave me also gall for my meat; and in my thirst they gave me vinegar to drink" (Psalm 69:21).

What was offered Christ at His crucifixion?

"They gave him vinegar to drink mingled with gall; and when he had tasted thereof, he would not drink" (Matthew 27:34; see also John 19:28-30).

With whom did the prophet Isaiah say Christ would make His grave?

"And he made his grave with the wicked, and with the rich in his death" (Isaiah 53:9).

With whom was Christ crucified?

"Then were there two thieves crucified with him, one on the right hand, and another on the left" (Matthew 27:38).

BURIEL AND RESURRECTION

Who took charge of Christ's body after it was taken down from the cross?

"A rich man of Arimathaea, named Joseph, ... went to Pilate, and begged the body of Jesus. ... He wrapped it in a clean linen cloth, and laid it in his own new tomb, which he had hewn out in the rock" (Matthew 27:57-60).

To what experience in the life of a noted prophet did Christ refer when speaking of the length of His stay in the grave?

"But he answered and said unto them, An evil and adulterous generation seeketh after a sign; and there shall no sign be given to it, but the sign of the prophet Jonas; for as Jonas was three days and three nights in the whale's belly; so shall the Son of man be three days and three nights in the heart of the earth" (Matthew 12:39, 40).

What prophecy foretold Christ's triumph over death?

"For thou wilt not leave my soul in hell; neither wilt thou suffer thine Holy One to see corruption" (Psalm 16:10; see Acts 2:24-27).

Appendix B

Did Jesus Rise From the Dead?
How A Trained Lawyer Looked at the Evidence

Lawyers are trained to be thorough in examining and sifting evidence. Often they can detect inconsistencies in testimony indicating fraud where ordinary observers are easily deceived.

Albert L. Roper, graduate of the University of Virginia (U.S.A.) and its law school, and a member of the Virginia State bar for many years, wrote a book in which he examines the evidence of Christ's death and resurrection from a lawyer's viewpoint (*Did Jesus Rise From the Dead?*, Grand Rapids, Michigan: Zondervan Publishing House, 1965). Following is a resumé of his book:

(1) The historical facts stated in the Gospel records confirm the life of Jesus in the time of Tiberius Caesar, emperor of Rome, and Pontius Pilate, Procurator of Judea under Roman rule. The roman historian Cornelius Tacitus (A.D. 55-120) vouches for the existence of "Christus, the founder of the name, [who] had undergone the death penalty in the reign of Tiberius, by sentence of the procurator Pontius Pilatus, and the pernicious superstition [of his teachings] was checked for a moment, only to break out once more, not merely in Judaea, the home of the disease, but in the capital itself" (*Histories*, XV. 44; translated

by Clifford H. Moore, vol. 4, pp. 283, 284; Cambridge, Mass.: Harvard University Press). Tacitus was an eminent and disinterested Roman historian, obviously an unbeliever; he recorded what was generally accepted at the time as fact, and his scholarly learning and accuracy were highly esteemed by contemporaries. No historical event of ancient times is more firmly established than that Jesus died. The enemies of the early followers of Jesus were numerous and powerful; the imperial government of Rome held tight control of practically the entire civilized world and her watchful police and military were everywhere. The unbelieving Jews were also everywhere, and powerful. To disprove either the death or the resurrection of Jesus would have smothered the early church in its cradle.

(2) The Roman Governor Pilate marveled that Jesus should die as early as "the ninth hour" of the day when it was usual for crucifixion victims to linger on for many hours, even some days. He sent for the Roman centurion to confirm the death. A Roman spear had been thrust through his side, and a stream of blood and water had flowed out (Mark 15:42-45; John 19:32-37). The testimony of the witnesses after the resurrection demonstrates that his body had indeed been thus mutilated. The enemies of Jesus and the disciples were so observant and determined that they would have made capital of any "Jesus" who survived the cross and hobbled around afterward with nail-pierced feet and hands and torn side; the fact is that not a shred of evidence was ever brought forth to support such a theory. Jesus' numerous enemies were as convinced of his death as were his friends. And none ever brought forward the suggestion that Jesus had escaped the actual crucifixion by a substitute taking his place at the last moment. Both the Roman guard and the determined Jewish priests who wanted revenge would have prevented it.

All the witnesses testify that Jesus appeared to them in a glorified, resurrected body.

(3) Governor Pilate had an Imperial Seal of Rome affixed to the stone that blocked the entrance to Jesus' tomb. No one would dare to tamper with such a Roman seal, under pain of death. This exposes the story concocted by the Jewish priests, that the disciples stole his body, as a lie. A lawyer looks for a motive that lies behind a crime. The terrified disciples who were too scared even to ask Pilate for the body of their Master would never dare to break an Imperial Roman seal in order to steal it. And they themselves did not even believe the resurrection was possible—why would they try to steal the body? The rich man's tomb (Joseph's, of Arimathea) was good enough for his burial; they could not provide a better one.

(4) The apostle John (chapter 20:1-10) tells simple, direct facts about what he saw in the empty tomb on the third day. If he were fabricating a tale in order to deceive, he would have embroidered the story with supernatural manifestations, as are so common in legends and "miracle" stories. Again, the other disciples "believed not" when the women who found the empty tomb told of the angels' words that he had been resurrected. They were hard-headed, mature men who were not subject to women's emotional tales. But something convinced these hard-headed men. What was it? Two things: they saw the resurrected Jesus and examined his nail-pierced hands and feet and torn side; and they became aware of the Old Testament prophecies that predicted this very death and resurrection of the Messiah.

(5) The testimony of the pagan Roman soldiers that Jesus had risen from the dead is unimpeachable. They were eyewitnesses (Matthew 28:11-15). Not even the enemies of Jesus doubted that the tomb was empty. They would not

have the slightest reason to steal his body, for they wanted to prevent a resurrection story; and the friends of Jesus could not steal it because the power of the greatest empire on earth was employed in guarding the tomb against just such a theft. Between ten and thirty Roman soldiers were detailed for the job. "Soldiers cold-blooded enough to gamble over a dying victim's cloak are not the kind of men to be hood-winked by timid Galileans or to jeopardize their Roman necks by sleeping on their posts." And thieves do not leave the scene of their crime in a neat, orderly condition as was the empty tomb, with the grave clothes folded and set properly in place. Thieves work in haste and leave things in disarray.

(6) *The idea that Jesus escaped actual crucifixion, and that a* substitute took his place while he went free, is contradicted by all the evidence. Such an idea involves Jesus in trickery and deceit, and everyone, including the honoured Koran, recognized that he was without sin. How could he convince eleven devoted disciples plus "five hundred" witnesses that he had risen from the dead, showing them scarred hands, feet, and side, if he had tricked someone else into taking his place on the cross? Someone would have recognized the fraud. People don't endure life-long suffering, loss of property, and finally death by torture in order to propagate a lie. And the character of the disciple witnesses is not that of deceitful plotters.

(7) *A lawyer is impressed by the behaviour of the disciples, who* for some important reason were transformed from cowardly, discouraged, even unbelieving adherents of a supposedly dead cause into the most bold witnesses possible to find. Says lawyer Roper: "The only reasonable explanation of the 'something' is, I submit, the truthfulness of the record given us. No other explanation explains."